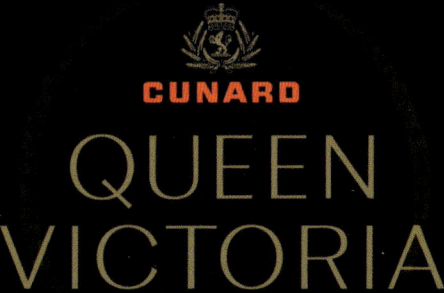

CUNARD

QUEEN VICTORIA

MILES COWSILL

Published by:

Ferry Publications, PO Box 33, Ramsey, Isle of Man IM99 4LP

Tel: +44 (0) 1624 898445   Fax: +44 (0) 1624 898449

E-mail: ferrypubs@manx.net   Website: www.ferrypubs.co.uk

Contents

Produced and designed by Ferry Publications trading as Lily Publications Ltd

PO Box 33, Ramsey, Isle of Man, British Isles, IM99 4LP

Tel: +44 (0) 1624 898446   Fax: +44 (0) 1624 898449

www.ferrypubs.co.uk   EMail: info@lilypublications.co.uk

Printed and bound by Gomer Press Ltd., Wales, UK +44 (0) 1559 362371 © Lily Publications 2017

First Published: May 2010, Second Edition: August 2010, Third Edition: May 2014

ISBN: 978-1-911268-13-0

Revised and Fourth Edition: October 2017

Foreword

BY CAPTAIN PETER PHILPOTT

It is difficult to believe that December 2017 will mark ten years since this remarkable ship entered service, after being named by Her Royal Highness The Duchess of Cornwall, who was accompanied by His Royal Highness the Prince of Wales.

I am writing this whilst *Queen Victoria* is not exactly looking her best as she sits in a dry dock in Palermo, Sicily, where she is undergoing a £34 million refit which will see 43 mid-ship cabins converted into Britannia Club staterooms with a dedicated Britannia Club Dining restaurant. The refurbished accommodation will include new carpets, soft furnishings, flat-screen TVs, as well as tea and coffee-making facilities. The ship's Grand Suites and Penthouse Suites are being redesigned, and a new Chart Room bar will be introduced. Five new Penthouse suites will feature floor-to-ceiling windows with defined living and sleeping spaces and bathrooms with natural light. And several existing public spaces will be lavishly redone.

This investment in *Queen Victoria* just goes to demonstrate Cunard's passion for delivering an experience that exceeds guests' expectations in luxury travel by sea and will ensure that *Queen Victoria* remains one of the most celebrated ships at sea. In fact she quickly established herself as a popular member of the Cunard fleet soon after entering service and is now the third largest Cunard ship ever built - she was the second largest when she entered service but her sister, *Queen Elizabeth*, assumed that position when she joined the fleet in 2010.

The *Queen Victoria* has never been about size superlatives – she is about style. When the designers of *Queen Victoria* began to consider the ship's interior public spaces, they drew on the well-recorded and rich history of previous Cunard ocean liners to set the tone. From the ship's double and triple-height spaces - a design feature of grand liners of the past - to rooms imbued with an elegant yet understated British charm, the overall effect is both contemporary and classically historic with some exciting innovations. These include the first traditional West End-style private viewing boxes at sea in the Royal Court Theatre, the first Cunardia exhibit display at sea, housing Cunard artefacts and memorabilia, and the first two-storey library at sea featuring an elegant spiral staircase.

I am delighted to write the foreword to this special book by Miles Cowsill just as I am delighted and privileged to be Master of this great ship as she resumes service in her tenth year and will be set to dazzle and delight many more passengers for many years to come.

Captain Peter Philpott
Master, Queen Victoria

INTRODUCTION

*The **Queen Victoria** making her way up the Amazon in 2017. She is the largest passenger ship to sail the Amazon between the dark Rio Negro and the pale Amazon to date. Captain*

This book is produced as one in a series of three titles on Cunard's four major ships of the 21st Century. The *Queen Victoria*, was constructed with the influence of *QE2* success and the many of those who loved this famous Scottish-built ship from 1967. The *Queen Victoria* was named by the Duchess of Cornwall at Southampton in late 2007; the five Cunard Queens prior to this have been launched or named by the Queens on the throne at the time of their building, with the *QE2*, the *Queen Mary 2* and the new *Queen Elizabeth* all being so honoured by the present reigning monarch.

This ship was built in the series of 'Vista' class vessels for Carnival Group, already operated within the group by Holland America, P&O, Costa and Cunard. The Italian shipbuilders Fincantieri worked closely together with Cunard to ensure that the *Queen Victoria,* and later her near sister the *Queen Elizabeth,* remained distinctively unique but also able to partner the Line's flagship *Queen Mary 2*.

While being sister ships of the same building class, the *Queen Victoria* and *Queen Elizabeth*, built three years apart, differ in much the same way that the first 'Mary' and 'Elizabeth' had their own very distinctive characters.

In many ways the *Queen Victoria* shows the same sort of refinement in detail over the *Queen Elizabeth* that distinguished the first 'Elizabeth' from the *Queen Mary*. The 'Victoria' shows a similarly gentle lightening of the overall interior palette over that of the 'Victoria' as her namesake of 70 years earlier had revealed in comparison with the *Queen Mary*.

The *Queen Victoria* has 16 decks, 12 of which are devoted to passengers. The public rooms are concenterd on Decks 2, 3, 9, 10 and 11 and occupy some 118,000 square feet. The theme of design for the vessel is the art deco era from the times of the first Cunard Queens. With a crew of 1,050, the cruise ship is like a 'mini town' to her guests.

On an average cruise of 14 days some 1 million pieces of glass and china are washed, 4,000 pints of beer and some days 5,250 bottles of wine and champagne are drunk. Some 10,000 meals are served a day on board to passengers and the crew and staff. On a turnround day in port, around 100,000 items have to be washed before embarking on another cruise.

This book traces a brief history of Cunard and the introduction in 1967 of the *QE2*, a firm favourite of many of the Cunard passengers and many regular guests today on the *Queen Victoria*. The *Queen Elizabeth 2* set new standards of travel for the sixties developing cruise market, which was to be the

...eter Philpott berthed the vessel at the port of Manaus, nearly 900 miles from the open ocean. ...Cunard)

hallmark of Cunard from the early seventies.

As Cunard marked 50 years since the naming of our much-loved liner *QE2* in September, and building on the success of the *Queen Victoria,* it was announced that they planned to build a third 'Vista class' ship, which will join the fleet during 2022. It will be the first time since 1999 that Cunard have had four ships in simultaneous service.

The publication also encompasses the 175th Anniversary celebrations of Cunard, including the three *Queens* rendezvous at Liverpool and earlier events at Southampton and Lisbon. The fourth edition also offers an update of her career since entering operations and includes an overview of her £34 million refit at Fincantieri Shipyard in Palermo, Italy in 2017, which included new cabins at her stern and upgrading of her accommodation. In addition Britannia Club Dining was introduced as part of the upgrade of her accommodation,

together with 43 spacious Britannia Club staterooms to match the other ships in fleet. As part of the refit all the staterooms were improved together with the Grand Suites. The popular Chart Room concept was upgraded as part of her overhaul on Deck 2, off the Grand Lobby, where Café Carinthia had been originally built. It is interesting to compare how design, fittings, colours and expectations have moved on over ten years, when you compare the internal photography to that in Chapters 3 as ordinally built, and the major design enhancements during 2017 in Chapter 5.

In this edition, I have introduced a wealth of new photographs to complement her ten years in service and her major refit in May 2017.

I would like to acknowledge the original author of this book, Philip Dawson, for all his research and hard work with the first three editions. Finally my thanks also go out to Peter Shanks, Lee Powell, Captain Peter Philpott, Michael Gallagher, Robert Lloyd, Sara Donaldson, Craig Dunn, Andrew Cooke, and all the staff and crew on the *Queen Victoria* who made me and my wife so welcome on board when we visited on the ship in May 2015 in Liverpool.

Miles Cowsill
Isle of Man
October 2017

CHAPTER 1

Setting the scene

Cunard's new *Queen Victoria* is the first to follow the great success of the Line's highly acclaimed liner *Queen Mary 2*, delivered at the end of 2003 as a new fleet mate, and ultimately a replacement, for the much-loved *Queen Elizabeth 2*, herself dating from 1969. While *Queen Victoria* incorporates much from the new *QM2*, with the benefit of her proven service experience in particular, the *Queen Victoria* is herself remarkably different in character, reflecting some of the Line's more traditional values, going back to the era of true grand-luxe sea travel from even earlier than the venerable old Queens, *Mary* and *Elizabeth*.

The *QE2* was originally built as a crisply modern expression of the very best in British architectural and interior design from the Swinging Sixties, during which she was planned. The *QM2* followed in a contemporary ocean-going hotelier style with, as her co-ordinating interior architect Andy Collier of SMC Design puts it, a 'tip of the hat to tradition'. The *Queen Victoria* presents a predominantly traditional on-board atmosphere, celebrating the popular notion of Cunard's illustrious history and background. Rather than endeavouring to reproduce period pieces from earlier times, generic classic styling in the public areas asserts the desired atmosphere as a background for enjoyment of the experience, in an otherwise entirely up-to-date cruise setting that meets today's lifestyle expectations.

The *Queen Victoria* is also a significant product of Carnival Corporate Shipbuilding, which serves the needs of the entire Carnival Group as the parent of Cunard, Holland America, Costa and Carnival's own brands, along with P&O and Princess Cruises. With this comes the world's greatest mass of passenger shipbuilding know-how and experience, covering all the latest technological advances in power and propulsion, navigation and electronics, energy conservation and environmental friendliness. While providing for the distinct culture and flavour of each fleet and individual ship,

*Top: The **Queen Mary** leaves Southampton for the last time. (John Hendy)*

*Above: The **Arcadia**, originally earmarked to become Cunard's **Queen Victoria**, in the event she was completed for P&O Cruises as the only Vista-class ship in their fleet. (Andrew Cooke)*

*The **QE2** in her short-lived post Falklands livery. (FotoFlite)*

*The **Queen Victoria** pictured shortly after her refit in 2017. This views shows the extension to the passenger accommodation at the stern. (Cunard)*

a highly rationalised approach has been built up to provide the all-important inner workings, such as food and beverages, hotel services and laundry, and stores and baggage handling, that go on behind the scenes away from the passengers' gaze. Headquartered in Southampton, England, this is a veritable dynamo of shipbuilding activity that traces its origins back to Carnival's first new ship, the *Tropicale*, completed nearly three decades ago in 1981.

In 2003, before the *QM2*'s inaugural season the following year, plans were already afoot at Carnival for the fourth hull in their upscale Vista class series, of which the lead ship *Zuiderdam* was delivered to Holland America Line in

November 2002, to be allocated to Cunard for completion in 2005 as part of a fleet redevelopment scheme to bring the Line into the same league as its competitors. Ultimately this ship ended up as P&O's *Arcadia*, with Cunard moving to a modified and slightly lengthened additional ship in the series, delivered as the *Queen Victoria* two years later at the end of 2007.

Built as Cunard's second largest vessel after the *QM2*, this would definitely be a Queen-class addition to the fleet, though without herself necessarily being a fully-fledged North Atlantic liner of the same power and structural stamina as the *QM2*. While the pundits speculated that

*Above: The **Queen Mary 2** and **QE2** pictured at Sydney. (Cunard)*

stalwart Cunard names such as *Mauretania*, *Aquitania* or perhaps even *Berengaria*, might be chosen, a Queen-sized Cunarder would have to be given a Queen's name, and thus it was that inevitably *Queen Victoria* came out on top as early as 2004 to be the most logical choice. The *QE2* was at the time still in service, with no immediate prospect of being sold off and mustered out of the fleet. While the name *QM2* acknowledges the old *Queen Mary*'s enduring sojourn in a static role as a hotel and tourist attraction in Long Beach, California, there would be no need to qualify the new ship's name with a numeral, either Roman or Arabic, as Victoria's name has never been used by Cunard nor for any other merchant ship currently in existence.

Yet as the management and technical talent at Carnival, Cunard and the ship's Italian builders Fincantieri, dealt with the business of designing and building the new Cunarder, their marketing colleagues started to promote the aura of the ultimate traditional cruise experience aboard an iconic Cunard liner to the cruising public. Probably no one at the time realised the significance of the long and illustrious reign of Queen Victoria, as the prosperous golden age into which the Cunard Line itself was born and lived through its adolescence.

A child of the Victorian era

Eighteen-year-old Alexandrina Victoria, daughter of Prince Edward Augustus, Duke of Kent and Princess Victoria of Saxe-Cobourg-Saalfeld, became Queen of Great Britain and its overseas possessions on the morning of 20th June 1837 following her uncle, King William IV's death at the age of 71 from heart failure at 2:00 am that day. The throne had passed to Victoria because neither her father, nor his two siblings, had any other surviving legitimate children at the time of William's death. Victoria's reign of 63 years and seven months, until her death on 22nd January 1901, was the longest in British history until Queen Elizabeth II came to the throne in 1952; this period of Victoria's reign was a time of great prosperity and human achievement known as the 'Victorian era'. As Britain had by then become a constitutional monarchy, where political and executive power is vested with an elected parliament whose prime minister generally advises the monarch on matters of government and state, the presence of Victoria and her Prince Consort, Albert, was an important rallying symbolic significance for the times.

The Victorian era also coincided with, and was part of, a broader phenomenon known as the Industrial Revolution, which brought about the greatest period of change experienced by human civilisation since the agricultural and Neolithic Revolution that defined the beginning of our civilisation more than 10,000 years ago. Starting in the early nineteenth century, a transition was made from an agrarian economy with manual labour and draft-animal power to mining and machine-based manufacturing, originating in the textile and iron industries. From about the time of Queen Victoria's coronation the so-called Second Industrial Revolution was focused more on the growth of mass transport systems by rail, sea, and later road, as well as the building of infrastructure and production of consumer goods and other manufactured products for domestic and export markets. Combined, the Second Industrial Revolution and Victorian era were a remarkable period driven largely by the march of great economic, scientific, technical, social and intellectual progress.

There was great engineering progress in steam power, mechanisation and in the fabrication of machinery and other structures of iron and steel that brought with it the development of railways and steam shipping. These quickly progressed from their infancy, as the technical curiosities

first created by their inventors, to become major industries and a way of life for many.

Transcontinental railways were built in Australia, Canada, the United States and across the subcontinent of India. The Suez Canal was built, creating a direct sea link between the Mediterranean and the Red Sea, greatly shortening the sailing distance from Britain and Europe to India, the Far East, Australia and New Zealand. Photography progressed from its experimental origins to the point where hand-held cameras and film processing were available to the public. Telegraph, and later wireless, brought about the vestigial beginnings of the real-time communications that are the basis of our networked and online world of the twenty-first century.

In 1839, two years after Victoria took the throne, Samuel Cunard (1787–1865), an enterprising Canadian merchant from Halifax, Nova Scotia, was awarded an Admiralty contract to carry transatlantic mail by steamship between Liverpool, Halifax and Boston, with scheduled sailings every two weeks in both directions for eight months of the year, for an annual fee of £50,000. Precedents had already been set for steam-powered Atlantic passages from as early as 1819, when the American paddle steamer *Savannah* crossed from the American city of Savannah to Liverpool in 27 days and 15 hours, during which her engines were only in use for 80 hours. Those earlier ventures with perhaps the best chance of being commercially viable were carried out by the British and American Steam Navigation Company and the Great Western Steamship Company, both founded in 1838, though remaining in service only until 1841 and 1846 respectively.

With steam there came a fundamental change in the shipping business, that vessels 'will positively sail full or not,' on scheduled dates, instead of the existing sailing packet practice of waiting for a full cargo before sailing. While there was no way to determine actual voyage times under sail, constant speeds could be maintained aboard machine-powered ships, and their comings and goings thus scheduled on the same basis as railway timetables.

Four wooden paddle steamers were launched on the Clyde for Cunard, each with a measure of 1,135 gross tons (GT), a length of 69.6 metres, a speed of 9 knots, and modest accommodation for 115 passengers. The first of these, *Britannia*, made her maiden voyage to Halifax and Boston with only 63 passengers aboard, sailing from Liverpool on 4th July 1840, arriving in Halifax 12 days and 10 hours later on 17th July. The remaining three ships, *Acadia*, *Caledonia* and *Columbia*, were completed and came on-stream between August that year and the following January, bringing into being a transatlantic passenger and mail service of great regularity and reliability, and originating the longest-serving passenger shipping enterprise in history, continuing to the present day with Atlantic voyages being made now aboard the Line's *Queen Mary 2*.

The company was originally chartered in Liverpool as the British and North American Royal Mail Steam Packet Company. This rather formal and somewhat unwieldy title was shortened to 'The Cunard' or simply Cunard in everyday usage, and has since formally become Cunard Line, or again simply Cunard.

While the volume of mail and numbers of passengers steadily increased, as did Cunard's competition from the American-flag Ocean Steam Navigation Company, and Inman and Collins Line, the size of the original *Britannia* and her sisters was tripled when the twin-funnelled *Persia* of 3,300 tons made her debut in 1856 as the world's then largest passenger steamer. The *Persia* and her later sister the *Scotia*, delivered six years later in 1862, had a unique romantic beauty about them, with the long sleek lines of their hulls and a beautifully balanced profile with their twin funnels

located equidistant fore and aft of the paddle-wheel enclosures. Apart from reclaiming the Atlantic Blue Riband honours for speed from their American competitors, *Persia* and *Scotia* also brought a vestigial sense of land-based hospitality and reassuring home comfort to the Cunard fleet.

From the sailing packet accommodation approach of Cunard's original *Britannia* and the slightly larger *Cambria* and *Hibernia* that had inaugurated Cunard's direct service between Liverpool and New York in 1848, where a single saloon served as the dining room and gathering place for all other social activity, the *Persia* and *Scotia* brought the added diversity of a library and smoking room. There were two saloons, forward and aft of the machinery spaces and funnels amidships, each with a cupola adding a sense of height and airiness to the interior. There were internal passages on the cabin deck bypassing the machinery spaces amidships, so that passengers could access all parts of the accommodations without having to go by way of the open decks, and for the first time, there was steam heating in the cabins themselves.

Such was the great march of engineering and technological progress that the *Persia* and *Scotia* were at the same time both the last paddle wheelers built for intercontinental service and pioneer iron-hulled ships. The *Persia* was also a notable pioneer of safety with her hull subdivided into seven watertight compartments and fitted with a double bottom beneath the coal bunkers and cargo holds. Iron soon gave way to steel hull construction and the paddle wheel's prominence was universally usurped by the underwater screw propeller, with the *China* of 1862 being Cunard's first propeller-driven Atlantic liner. These developments changed the appearance and indeed the internal layout of ships, and provided for them to be built in greater sizes with more carrying capacity and higher speeds.

Perhaps of even greater significance is the fact that the mid 1850s-built *Jura* and *Etna* were the first Cunarders to have steerage-class accommodations, which were fitted in 1860. Although the *Jura* and *Etna* were sold the following year, new Cunard passenger ships from 1860 onwards were built with steerage accommodations to serve the growing transatlantic exodus of émigrés to Canada and the United States. The *Russia*, which entered service in 1867 had accommodation for 150 in cabin class and 800 in third or steerage.

The nineteenth century's latter half produced one of the greatest birth booms in history, with the population of England nearly doubling from 16.8 million in 1851 to 30.5 million in 1901. People flocked to the cities in search of employment, while the more pastoral ways of life were in decline. Many of those who were fortunate enough to find employment had to live in appalling squalor, with children having to work long hours at menial tasks to help support their families. Furthermore the 1851 census revealed demographic gender imbalance with four per cent more women than men, ostensibly contributing to the widespread urban expansion of 'The Great Social Evil,' as prostitution was then euphemistically referred to by genteel do-gooders. Some 15 million Britons, of both genders and in all walks of life, found that their best option was to seek new lives for themselves and their families overseas in Canada, the United States and Australia.

At the same time Cunard's competitors from across the Channel, such as Hamburg America Line, North German Lloyd and French Line, were, in addition to their own first and cabin trades, likewise conveying Europe's disenchanted and displaced to the New World's more hospitable shores. In 1871 the Liverpool-based White Star Line emerged to become one of Cunard's most formidable competitors, before the two rival lines were amalgamated during the 1930s. The North Atlantic steamship lines in particular were quick to realise that carrying large numbers of people in

*Top: The **Britannia** arriving at Liverpool in 1840. (Cunard)*

*Above: The **Arabia** was built in 1852. She was involved in the Crimean War and also carried Cunard's first royal passenger. (Cunard)*

Top: Sir Samuel Cunard shortly before his death in his London home at the age of 78 in 1865. (Cunard)

*Above: The **Umbria** was the last of the twentieth century liners to carry sails. (Cunard)*

basic accommodation with rudimentary service brought an economy of scale that was highly lucrative. About a hundred years later, when the Boeing 747 jumbo jet started to fly, the airline industry was to again discover the good fortunes of mass travel.

The pursuit of prestige and speed continued to flourish, and to form the basis of competition and loyalties for wealthy and influential passengers, though the cost of providing the creature comforts of first and cabin classes and the shortest possible passage times was to some degree underwritten by the great masses crowding the lower decks.

Over the final decades of the Victorian era huge strides were made in shipbuilding and marine engineering, as the paddle wheel gave way first to the single screw propeller and then to twin screws, and the original side lever engine was replaced by more powerful and fuel-efficient compound multiple-cylinder piston machinery. While Cunard was under contract to the Admiralty for carrying the Royal Mail, before this responsibility was transferred to the Postmaster General in 1867, the Line often found itself restricted by the Royal Navy's rather conservative approach to innovation in shipbuilding and marine engineering. Advances such as screw propellers and compound engines were only adopted by the Admiralty after very careful evaluation and testing.

As the *Persia* was being planned, for instance, the Admiralty had reluctantly agreed to the use of iron for the ship's hull, despite having banned its use for mail steamers on the basis of concern for suitability in naval service if the ship were to be requisitioned as an auxiliary in wartime, though they insisted that she be paddle-wheel driven, still believing this to be the more reliable means of propulsion.

Cunard was thus at the competitive disadvantage of being bound to navy design and building standards in the interest of safeguarding the 'swift, regular and safe passage' of Her Majesty's mails. Yet at a time when an ocean crossing was still considered risky, Cunard's outstanding safety record and reputation for regular and punctual service embodied the comfortably secure ideal of swift, safe regular passage, even where their competitors were technologically ahead of them. It is perhaps this point more than anything else that lies behind the mystique of Cunard's tradition that prevails to this day.

The Victorian era's final and greatest triumph of marine engineering was the steam turbine that made possible the building of much larger and faster ships and was the main source of propulsion for ships until well into the latter half of the twentieth century. The turbine's first working prototype was audaciously shown off by its inventor, Charles Algernon Parsons (1854–1931), who virtually stole the show at the 1897 Spithead Naval Review honouring Queen Victoria's Diamond Jubilee by dexterously piloting his own yacht *Turbinia* around the Royal Yacht *Victoria and Albert*, the lines of British and visiting foreign warships and other naval vessels. Built for testing and demonstrating the compact and high-performing steam turbine, the *Turbinia* that day maintained the unprecedented speed of 34.5 knots – too fast even for the Royal Navy patrol boat dispatched to chase her away.

Realising that the navies of other marine powers such as France and Germany would no doubt be swift to adopt this new marvel, the Admiralty was quick to respond. The Royal Navy's first turbine-powered destroyers, the *HMS Cobra* and the *HMS Viper*, were commissioned two years later in 1899. In the twentieth century's opening years, Cunard started planning for the turbine-powered *Lusitania* and *Mauretania* to be the largest and fastest liners in the world when simultaneously completed in 1907. Cautious as ever, though, the Line first had turbine machinery installed in 1905 aboard the *Carmania*, the second of two otherwise near-identical ships, so that the new machinery's performance could be

reliably assessed against the conventionally engined sister ship *Caronia*. Thus, as the Cunard Line came of age, so to speak, at the Victorian era's close in 1901 this final great engineering advance of that epoch set the pace for steam propulsion over the following 70 years.

Hotel at sea

Along with world industrialisation, there also came far greater personal mobility thanks mainly to the railways, the steamship and later the automobile. Although then still too expensive for the great masses, those who could afford it or needed to move about could cover far greater distances in much less time. Travel became a regular necessity of trade and commerce, as raw materials had to be purchased and brought to the manufacturing centres and finished products, including the first consumer goods available to the emerging middle class, were brought to market throughout the land and overseas.

By the late Victorian era, Great Britain and continental Europe were already covered by extensive rail networks, and transcontinental rail services were already operating across North America, Australia and the Indian subcontinent. Steamship service to just about anywhere in the world was regular and reliable, and for those travelling from Britain and Europe to Asia and the Antipodes the voyage was significantly shortened thanks to the Suez Canal. One could travel under steam power, for instance, from central Europe to the Pacific Rim by rail and sea, without having to sail around Cape Horn or cross the Isthmus of Panama, with forward bookings and hotel reservations all being secured ahead of time by telegraph.

With all of this came the first large urban or Grand Hotels, built by the railways as an adjoining part of their city terminus stations, as in the London examples of the

*The **Lucania**, like the **Campania** had a remarkably clean-lined and modern appearance, for her day, being among the first Cunarders to do away with the auxiliary sailing rig and dispense with the centre mast and its rigging altogether. (Author's collection)*

Paddington Hotel and St. Pancras Hotel. Like factories and other industrial structures, the railway station and Grand Hotel were a new architectural genre of the age, as the international airport terminal and shopping mall were to develop as new building types of the twentieth century.

As steamships became larger and faster, and inevitably more comfortable, their rival owners began to visualise themselves as much as being in the ocean-going hotel business, at least for first class, as they were purveyors of transport from one place to another.

Hotelism, as it was then called, in effect offered those of the emerging middle class an opportunity for a few days at least, either on dry land or at sea, to live it up in the style of the wealthy in opulent surroundings, with fine food, beverages and cigars, the companionship of other guests in the public rooms, and an abundance of personal service from obliging staff. For the filthy rich it at least maintained the standards they were already accustomed to in their own country homes or townhouses, usually with the added benefit that they could bring along their own valets, butlers and chamber maids, for whom guest staff accommodation was provided.

Without themselves being the pioneers of significantly higher standards of service and comfort on the North

Atlantic, Cunard's *Umbria* and *Etruria* of 1884–1885 were nonetheless notable trend setters as veritable sea-going hotels. Following the example of the railway Grand Hotels on terra firma, the idea here was to offer the traveller or passenger a sense of celebration of the voyage itself with fine cuisine, accommodation and service at least as good as, if not better than, they could expect at their country estates and private clubs ashore, all within the special milieu of the shipboard life and the by then far more comfortable experience of getting from one place to another.

First- and cabin-class passenger accommodations aboard the *Umbria* and *Etruria* were arranged throughout four decks, with walk-around outer promenades at two levels. The first-class public rooms included a spacious dining saloon, used only at meal times, along with a doughnut-shaped music salon on the deck above surrounding a domed central opening through the dining saloon ceiling, a large gentlemen's smoking room, and ladies' lounge and boudoir, along with various vestibules and foyers, a barber shop and other services. The ornate furnishing and almost excessive outfitting and decoration of these ships in its reflection of high Victorian affluence rightfully earned them their wide acclaim as 'floating hotels'.

The twin-propeller *Campania* and *Lucania* of 1893 surpassed 10,000 tons in size at 12,950 tons each, and were the first to be built without an auxiliary sailing rig as a backup contingency in case the machinery should fail. Apart from the inevitable refinements to the passenger amenities, which for the first time included deckchair rental and cabins for single travellers, the interior decoration was of acknowledged Elizabethan, Italian Renaissance and other period styles.

When the *Lusitania* and *Mauretania*, followed in 1907 as Cunard's first two true superliners, period styling of the first- and cabin-class passenger interiors had already set a

Top: The **Aquitania** *departs from Liverpool on her maiden voyage in May 1914. (Cunard)*

Above: *A deck scene on the* **Mauretania** *taken during her early career with the company. (Cunard)*

comfortable traditionalist standard for the Line's shipboard architecture. It was elegant and entirely liveable, rendered in an entirely human scale without being outsized, ostentatious or overpowering. The style reflected values that passengers would be at home and familiar with through its similarity with the design of hotels ashore such as the new Ritz Hotels in Paris and London, The Dorchester or New York's Waldorf Astoria. This was also the style of upper-class establishments such as The Athenian and Royal Automobile Club and the executive offices of financial, commercial and industrial enterprises on both sides of the Atlantic.

Publicity literature, books and magazines of the day often referred to interior decoration of this type, either ashore or afloat, as being typical of a 'stately British country home'. Those elements or artefacts of Elizabethan, Italian Renaissance or Louis XVI still to be found in the gentry's country houses existed from those times when the houses were either built or extensively modified and reflected the whim and fancy of their owners, recalling perhaps their travels abroad. The art of institutional period revival that was reaching its zenith in the twentieth century's opening years was scholarly design work carefully devised to assert an atmosphere of *bon vivant* in the commercially motivated surroundings of ships, hotels or private clubs. It was never to convey any theme or notion that was too profound or severe, but rather to assert a pleasing background of classical flourishes and whimsy for the enjoyment of modern twentieth-century living without being reminded of anything too lofty or serious.

With the greater size and complexity of the *Lusitania* and *Mauretania* and the added design sophistication of their passenger accommodations, Cunard engaged professional architects for the first time to co-ordinate the design and decoration of the first-class public spaces along with the deluxe cabins and suites. James Miller (1860–1947), whose experience included hotels, public buildings, rail and underground stations in the west of Scotland, was commissioned for the *Lusitania* and prominent London residential architect Harold A. Peto (1854–1933) for the *Mauretania*. Although neither had any ship design experience, nor had hotel design by then emerged as a specialty, the results they achieved were truly outstanding.

While the two ships were nearly identical in structure, engineering and layout, the interior architecture and decoration of each was unique. Peto's work aboard the *Mauretania* drew mainly on historic French influences, as the choice of these ashore had become fashionable in upper-class circles on both sides of the Atlantic, reflecting an apparent understanding of French interior decorating styles among the wealthy and well educated. The ship's double-height domed main dining room was decorated in a sixteenth-century François I style, panelled in dark Austrian oak, and the main lounge in a Louis XVI style with mahogany panelling and marble columns. Miller's Louis XVI *Lusitania* dining room used enamelled white panelling with gilded detailing and a Georgian style prevailed throughout her main suite of public rooms. The differing decorative schemes served best for passengers to distinguish one ship from the other as other differing structural detail in the superstructure fronts and ventilator cowls were probably too esoteric to be noticed by most passengers.

The *Lusitania* and *Mauretania* handily achieved their competitive objective of wresting the Blue Riband honours from North German Lloyd's *Deutschland* of 1899, only to face a different sort of challenge, mainly from Hamburg America and White Star, which were stressing higher standards of hotel luxury and service rather than speed records. White Star's *Olympic* and Hamburg America's *Imperator,* delivered in 1911 and 1913, were both very large ships for the time with high superstructures housing large numbers of luxury rooms and suites and extensive suites of opulent public rooms surrounded by glass-enclosed promenades. Cunard responded with the 45,647-ton *Aquitania* completed shortly before the outbreak of World War I in 1914.

Design of the *Aquitania*'s interiors was co-ordinated by the Parisian hotel architect Charles Mevès (1860–1914), by then noted for his designs of the Paris and London Ritz Hotels, and his English partner Arthur Davis (1878–1951). Mevès and Davis had already designed the Ritz-style first-class interiors for Hamburg America Line's *Amerika* of 1905, and Mevès had since been commissioned for the interiors of the *Imperator* and *Vaterland* to be handled by a German collaborator, Alphonse Bischoff, through his own practice in Cologne. By this arrangement Mevès could in effect work with the two competing steamship lines so long as there was no direct exchange of details between Davis and Boscoff, or through Mevès. Cunard had in fact approached Mevès and Davis in 1905 to design interiors for the *Lusitania* and *Mauretania*, though at the time they were already committed to their *Amerika* commission.

Widely known as 'The Ship Beautiful', Cunard's *Aquitania* was probably the finest period revivalist work done by Mevès and Davis, and certainly their last as Charles Mevès himself died the same year as her delivery. The various period styles used throughout the *Aquitania*'s public rooms were in many instances based on specific places ashore, with the smoking room, for instance, being adapted from a Charles II-period hall at Greenwich Hospital, and the main lounge modelled after the work of Sir Christopher Wren, reflecting his use of classic columns and entablature, and preference for classic white wall surfaces. A Brothers Adam style was chosen for the drawing room, domed deck entrance and reception room and long gallery. The writing room and an elegant ladies' lounge were in Louis XVI style. These and numerous

*Above: The Tourist Class Dining Room on the **Aquitania**. (Cunard)*

Below: Cunard's imposing headquarters on Liverpool's Pier Head. (Cunard)

Top: The **Laconia** *was built in 1921, she made her maiden voyage on 25th May 1922 from Southampton to New York. (University of Liverpool Cunard archive)*

Above: The Tourist Class Dining Room on the **Aquitania**. *(University of Liverpool Cunard archive)*

other styles were used for the first-class cabins and suites.

As delightfully old world as this was, it nonetheless reflected the best in modern hotel architecture at the time. The *Aquitania* was herself an otherwise entirely modern ship, with entirely contemporary standards of hotel comfort and service. The cabins in particular reflected a standard at par with the best hotels on land, featuring large rectangular rooms with full-sized bedsteads and many of these having separate en-suite bathrooms and lavatories. For Cunard, the *Aquitania* probably best represented the values of traditional hospitality and service and the notion of 'swift, regular and safe passage' upon which the Line and its enviable reputation was built. In the decades to follow, it would seem that perhaps the *Aquitania* embodied a personality that Cunard was reluctant to compromise to the whims of architectural and design modernists or perhaps also even to changing lifestyles.

Flirting with moderne

Before the outbreak of World War I in August 1914, Hamburg America Line showed that year, at the Werkbund Exhibition in Cologne, mock-up ship interiors of a simpler neo-classical style intended to set a new design direction for the Line's ships. The same exhibition also featured railway sleeper compartments and dining cars kitchen and serving facilities that were to greatly influence apartment design in the post-war age, with compact plans making wide use of built-in fixtures and furnishings. In light of these developments and their inevitable influences also on ship design, Victorian-era revivalist styles with their excessive artistic flourishes and curlicues were already becoming passé.

Another exhibition 11 years later, this one the *Exposition Internationale des Arts Industrielles et Décoratifs*, which ran through the summer of 1925 in post-World War I Paris, served to assert the great influences of modern twentieth-century design and art throughout the Western world. The French Line's new transatlantic liner *Ile de France* in effect brought the Exposition to New York on her maiden voyage two years later through her stunningly modern interior and decorative design. The ship was a veritable showcase of French moderne created by many of the same people whose work had featured prominently at the Exposition. These featured modern indirect and concealed lighting and an abundant use of mirrored glass, glossy veneers and bright metallic surfaces with soft furnishings in bold saturated colours and a great wealth of contemporary French art.

The *Ile de France* was followed by other ships reflecting the modern architecture and design of other nations, including Sweden's *Kungsholm* of 1928, Germany's rakish record-breaking *Bremen* and *Europa* at the end of the decade and Italy's fashionably modern 1932 *Conte di Savoia*. The ultimate expression of this genre was French Line's magnificent *Normandie* completed in 1935 as the first of the liner era's three great 80,000-ton superships. Decoratively, the *Normandie* was a sophisticated refinement of the *Ile de France*, rendered by many of the same designers, yet arranged on an axial plan that offered broad vistas through a remarkable series of open plan public rooms of double height.

Cunard, whose own superliner the *Queen Mary* was due to make her debut in 1936, had in the meantime kept up its own express North Atlantic service with the *Mauretania*, *Aquitania* and *Berengaria*, the former *Imperator* acquired in reparation for the *Lusitania*'s loss during World War I. While these ships had all undergone extensive modernisation refits, including conversion from coal to oil firing of their boilers and substantial upgrading of their cabin accommodations, mainly to provide greater numbers of cabins with en-suite toilets and baths, the *Mauretania*'s Harold Peto public

*Top: An evening scene after dinner on the **Aurania**. (Cunard)*

*Above: The **Mauretania**, **Normandie**, **Queen Mary** and **Queen Elizabeth** in New York on 7th March 1940 after the latter's secret Atlantic dash. (University of Liverpool Cunard archive)*

Life on board Cunarders

Days spent on board Cunard ships offered all types of entertainment, from tug of war matches to boxing on the upper deck. For those wanting just to take in the sea air a steward was always at hand for drinks or tea. Evening dress, cocktails and food made for that special Cunard evening.

*The **Queen Mary** arrives at Southampton after another crossing from New York. (Cunard)*

interiors and those of Mevès and Davis aboard the *Aquitania* and *Berengaria* remained largely unaltered as the Line's enduring house style.

While it would seem that Cunard itself, along with its regular clientele, was happy enough with the design status quo and content to leave moderne to the Europeans, concern was expressed within design circles as to whether the new, then still unnamed, Cunard superliner could be expected to portray a more appropriately contemporary impression of British design progress.

An illustrated editorial feature in the prestigious professional periodical *The Architects' Journal* pointed out that while hospitality ashore had generally progressed to a far more contemporary style of, for instance, the fashionable new Morecomb Hotel, the British liner was still caught in a

time warp of 'the dear old Waldorf'. It went on to ask that if the new Cunard was to have one of those names from the old Roman provinces ending in 'ia,' could it at least please be something closer to Contemporania that we may be seen abroad as being something more than merely 'a nation of olde-worlde shopkeepers?'

Arthur Davis was commissioned to co-ordinate the interior design of hull number 534, that was to be launched as the *Queen Mary*, in league with New York architect Benjamin Wistar Morris to advise on American style and taste. Like Davis, Morris's background was in the Beaux Arts style, and his work ashore had included Cunard's Manhattan offices, designed in a similar style to Mevès and Davis's work on the Line's headquarters at Liverpool's Pier head, dating from 1916. The *Queen Mary*'s structural design and internal

A wonderful view of the **Queen Elizabeth** *leaving the Solent for New York. (Ferry Publications Library)*

layout was fairly conventional, drawing upon the proven success of ships such as *Aquitania*. The architectural design and decoration was drawn from contemporary British and American influences that reflected the times of its creation, but inevitably lacked *Normandie*'s Gallic panache and grande gesture. While this came as something of a disappointment to some, it was nonetheless consistent with Cunard's own traditional ideals of 'swift, regular and safe passage' in the luxury of the world's biggest liner and ultimately proved to be commercially successful.

The *Queen Elizabeth* completed four years later in 1940, and only inaugurated in transatlantic passenger service after the end of World War II, was similar in overall design concept, outfitting and interior decoration. Structurally she was, however, considerably more modern, with two, rather than three, funnels and with the ventilation intakes concentrated around the bases of these, as was done with the *Normandie*, resulting in a likewise more straightforward layout of her public rooms with greater openness of plan. Benjamin Morris was again engaged to handle the interior design, this time working with George Grey Wornum as his British counterpart. Wornum was noted for his design of the Royal Incorporation of British Architects (RIBA) headquarters in Portland Place in London. The *Queen Elizabeth*'s interiors were a little less eclectic than those of the earlier ship, showing a higher degree of architectural correctness akin to the RIBA building.

Until planning was started in the mid 1950s for ships that would eventually replace the Queens, a number of smaller intermediate-class liners were built for service on Cunard's

Top left: First Class Main Hall on the **Queen Elizabeth**. (University of Liverpool Cunard archive)

Left: The **Queen Elizabeth** First Class Main Lounge. (University of Liverpool Cunard archive)

Above: Games deck on the **Queen Elizabeth** as she crosses the Atlantic. (University of Liverpool Cunard archive)

Top: Sir James Bisset and the Bell Boys on the **Queen Elizabeth.**
(University of Liverpool Cunard archive)

Above: Telephone switchboard on the **Queen Elizabeth** *- a far-cry from communications today. (University of Liverpool Cunard archive)*

Canadian route to Montréal, reflecting a post-World War II trend towards smaller ships with greater emphasis on tourist-class accommodations to meet the needs of that era's emigration boom. The interiors of these were designed in an eclectic style described by the Line as 'recreating the past in terms of the present by using modern methods of construction'. It was a somewhat overdressed style that seemed to be focused on reminiscences of a past that never really ever existed – it disappeared by the mid 1960s when two of the ships were redecorated in a more genuinely contemporary mode for cruising and the others were sold.

Meanwhile the Queens virtually became 1930s revivalist pieces in their own time as their interior architecture aged gracefully into settings reminiscent of a bygone era in grand-luxe travel when great ocean liners catered to Hollywood film stars, sports celebrities, business tycoons and even heads of state, most of whom had since taken to air travel. Famed also for their war service, these great and grand old ships became veritable institutions that upheld, especially for Americans, the romantic traditional notion of Britain and all things British. For Britons this also upheld a special cultural relationship with ships and the sea, stressing the more traditional maritime milieu of veneer panelled interiors with leather-upholstered smoking room club chairs and teak-planked open decks where one could still promenade and breath the sea air. The effect of all these factors was then heightened all the more by its stark contrast with the modernity of leading foreign post-war ships such as America's final Blue Riband champion *United States*, Holland America's elegant new *Rotterdam* and the 1950s haut moderne of the French Line's elite *France*.

Yet in the 1960s, when Cunard was planning for the ship that would eventually be launched as the *Queen Elizabeth 2*, Britain and all things British had suddenly become hip, cool and mod as the nation was swept by a revolution in pop that took the whole Western world by storm. There was a remarkable universality in the catchy upbeat music of sixties rock bands such as the Beatles and the Rolling Stones, and in the bright, simple and affordable fashions of the day such as the Mary Quant mini skirt and Barbara Hulanicki's flowing Biba styles that appealed to all ages, nationalities and classes and was as at home in Britain's suburban new towns such as Stevenage, Basildon and Hemel Hempstead, as it was in London, New York, Paris or Milan.

Cunard too became caught up in the tempo of the times, as the *QE2* was to emerge as a veritable icon of twentieth century British modernity at its absolute best. It had taken lobbying on the part of the architectural and industrial design professions, with questions even being asked in Parliament as to why what was to become Britain's merchant flagship should represent anything less than the nation's absolute best in her design and artistic decoration. As had been done with the old Queens, the new ship was being built with Crown loan guarantees and thus entitling the state and ultimately the taxpayers to have their say in the matter. With the Design Council's help a design team was put together for the new Cunarder that included prominent people who were progressive and forward looking, though without being too radical. Their modernist approach to realising this commission would reference the social and technological progress of the jet and space age, with new materials and aesthetics of the times.

The team was headed by James Gardner (1907–1995), responsible for the ship's exterior design and styling, and Dennis Lennon (1919–1991) heading a carefully selected cadre of prominent architects and designers who would create her myriad public interiors, suites and cabins. These included Professor Misha Black (1910–1977) and Sir Hugh Casson (1910–1999) who had previously worked with Gardner on designing the pavilions, structures and exhibits

Top: The **Ivernia** *under construction at John Brown & Co. She was built in 1955 as one of the four Saxonia class ships. (Cunard)*

Above: The **Carinthia** *was built for the transatlantic passenger service between the UK and Canada. (Cunard)*

Top: The **Mauretania** in Southampton Water. (FotoFlite)

Above: The **Queen Elizabeth 2** pictured in her advanced stage of building in the summer of 1967 shortly before her launching. (Bruce Peter collection)

for the 1951 Festival of Britain exhibition and had also worked on modern ship interiors for P&O Orient Lines.

At the time of her debut in the spring of 1969 the *QE2* provided a substantial glimpse into the future of luxury worldwide cruising. Apart from her stunningly attractive modern exterior lines and crisply contemporary interiors, the ship herself was in fact designed primarily for cruising without class barriers, with her alternative role in transatlantic service for two loosely segregated classes of service being secondary. As far as possible passenger accommodations were pushed outwards towards the sides of the ship to reduce the number of inside cabins to the barest minimum and to concentrate the public rooms, including the restaurants, on the uppermost decks where these would have the greatest exposure to natural light and direct access to the outer decks. Sir Hugh Casson described the ship as being 'an hotel on its head: four decks of public rooms of great variety of size and character, above five decks of bedrooms'.

Among the ship's most outstanding public spaces were the Queens Room, with its backlit latticed ceiling, elegant trumpet-shaped columns and bold wood-block wall panelling, the Double Room designed around a double-deck central space with a wide sweeping curved staircase joining its upper and lower levels and the circular main entrance foyer panelled in dark smoky veneers beneath a serrated fibreglass ceiling, devised to create the impressions of the concentric ripples created by dropping a stone into a pond. The cabins and suites had more of the look of modern hotel rooms, close carpeted throughout and all with their own en-suite toilets.

The shipbuilding journal *Shipbuilding and Shipping Record* hailed *QE2* as 'A ship with a past and a future,' looking back to Cunard's then nearly 130 years of liner experience and forward to the dawning of a new era in luxury worldwide cruising – with the *QE2* the Line almost immediately became a leader and innovator in cruise ships. Indeed deluxe cruise ships such as the *Sea Venture* and *Royal Viking Star* clearly showed the *QE2*'s direct influence in their design.

On board with Carnival

In 1998 Cunard became part of, and indeed was in effect rescued by, the Carnival Group. In the nearly three decades that had passed since the *QE2*'s debut, the Line had only taken delivery of two pairs of much smaller purpose-built new cruise ships in the 1970s and had subsequently acquired the former Norwegian America Line *Sagafjord* and *Vistafjord* as more suitable smaller running mates for *QE2* in luxury world-side cruising, with the *Vistafjord* later being renamed *Caronia*. Meanwhile, Carnival Cruises and other pioneers of modern-era cruising such as Royal Caribbean and Norwegian Caribbean, along with Cunard's old liner-era companions Costa, Holland America and P&O, were aggressively building ever larger fleets of spectacular new cruise ships.

Since 1971, Cunard had been owned by Trafalgar House, a large and diverse British conglomerate, which otherwise had no particular focus on shipping and shipbuilding. During this period the *QE2* went through numerous refits, refurbishments and reconfigurations, as well as a complete re-engining in 1986–1987, all aimed at retaining her position of great prestige against ever increasing competition. More and more the public's perception of Cunard was becoming that it primarily supported the *QE2* as its one and only ship in the size league of its competition, with the *Sagafjord* and *Vistafjord/Caronia* being viewed as but lesser secondary fleet mates despite the high standard of their accommodation and service. A new Queen code-named 'Q5' was proposed during the 1990s but was still on the drawing board by the time Carnival acquired Cunard.

Plans needed to be laid for the gracefully ageing *QE2*'s eventual replacement with a new cruise-oriented North

*Top: The **Queen Elizabeth 2**'s modern Double Room was originally fitted with a wide semi-circular staircase that was a key focal point of the room opposite its bandstand. (Bruce Peter collection)*

*Above: The **Queen Elizabeth 2**'s Columbia Restaurant was entered from a raised podium incorporated into the midships stairway enabling passengers to make a grand descent to their tables at mealtimes. (Miles Cowsill)*

Atlantic liner. Fleet mates of similar size and comparable prestige would also be needed to further develop and expand the unique Cunard product on the same basis as other cruise brands of a similarly traditional origin, such as Costa, Holland America and P&O. With the immense popularity and devoted regular following of the *QE2,* as probably the world's best-known and most-loved liner of all times, the Cunard brand was sure to be a sound bet for Carnival. For Cunard, there was the great advantage of being adopted by a new corporate parent with the resources to build on the grand scale needed to bring its long and illustrious history into a third century of its existence.

Carnival itself traces its own origins to a rather shaky start in 1972 as a one-ship operation when Canadian Pacific's redundant *Empress of Canada* was purchased for a knock-down price, deadheaded to Miami and hurriedly put into cruise service as is. Legend has it that there was only enough paint on board to partly cover the Canadian Pacific multimark funnel insignia, turning it into a stylised letter C that has remained ever since as the Carnival logo. Meanwhile, tickets for a short introductory cruise to Puerto Rico were being sold on Miami Beach for as little as ten dollars apiece. Renamed *Mardi Gras*, the ship suffered the unfortunate embarrassment of grounding on a sandbar in the Government Cut on her way out to sea from the Port of Miami's Dodge Island pier, though fortunately she was later re-floated undamaged. The preview cruise was ultimately a success and set the pace for Carnival's initial success in inexpensive and informal mass-market Caribbean cruising.

Two additional liners were acquired during the 1970s, including the Greek Line *Queen Anna Maria*, originally Canadian Pacific's *Empress of Britain* of 1956, and Safmarine's *SA Vaal*, delivered in 1961 to Union Castle Line as the *Transvaal Castle*. Musicians from the original *Empress of Canada* ship's orchestra, who had signed on with Carnival, recalled

that this had always been a very happy ship both for passengers and crew, inspiring the new owners to change their branding idea from 'The Golden Fleet' to 'The Fun Ships,' a name that aptly defined Carnival's core product, its development and identity for many years to come.

In 1980 Carnival's Danish-built *Tropicale* was the first in a spate of new cruise ships in the then large over 30,000-ton range, followed almost immediately by the more upscale Home Lines *Atlantic*, HAPAG-Lloyd *Europa* and Holland America *Nieuw Amsterdam* and *Noordam*. Compared with these, *Tropicale* made a far less traditional impression with her rakish lines, big gull-winged funnel, somewhat resembling the tail of a Boeing 727 airliner and her crooked row of cascading porthole-style windows following the gradual slope of the show-lounge floor inside, all of which were to become trademark Carnival features. The *Tropicale* was followed mid decade by the 45,000-ton *Holiday* and her two slightly larger sister ships *Celebration* and *Jubilee* from the Cockums yard in Sweden. Through the 1990s the Carnival fleet grew exponentially with the addition of eight Finnish-built 70,000-ton ships in the Fantasy series.

With the great success of its own brand, Carnival was looking to diversify into the more upscale league of other lines such as Holland America, Princess Cruises and Royal Viking Line. While the company's Project Tiffany was aimed at expanding into this market sector under a new brand of its own, the decision was finally made to instead absorb an upscale cruise line with an already established product and existing clientele, with Holland America Line being acquired by Carnival in 1989. Holland America was to retain its own name and much of its unique character and national identity, while at the same time fulfilling Carnival's objective of diversifying into the upscale cruise market and benefiting from the vast technical resources and extensive shipbuilding activity of its new owners.

*The **Queen Elizabeth 2** at sea following her conversion to diesel power, with her Quarter and Upper Decks extended aft and the stockier funnel in traditional Cunard colours needed for the diesel uptakes. (FotoFlite)*

Existing plans for two new Holland American ships were scrapped, with the *Statendam*, designed and built under the direction of Carnival's own technical department and delivered three years later in 1992. With luxury accommodation for 1,266 passengers in lower berths only and a measure of 55,000 tons, she was the first in a series of four ships, followed by the slightly larger *Rotterdam* and two additional ships in her league towards the decade's end.

With Cunard's 1998 acquisition, Carnival had absorbed probably the most prestigious name in the passenger shipping and cruise industry. Even though by then the *QE2*'s accommodations and amenities were in some regards no longer state-of-the-art, the aura of her unique singularity and the traditions behind her existence held tremendous trading value and public appeal. What needed to be done was to sustain these values through new generations of ships that would ultimately replace the world renowned and much-loved existing flagship.

Already named *Queen Mary 2* at an early stage of her planning, the new Cunard transatlantic liner was the only ship to be planned and built under Carnival's direction as a unique one-of-a-kind entity since *Tropicale* was delivered

*Top: In October 1983 the **Vistafjord** joined the Cunard fleet together with her sister ship **Sagafjord**. (FotoFlite)*

*Above: The **QE2** arrives in the Clyde on her farewell trip around the British Isles. (Miles Cowsill)*

some two decades earlier. As Cunard's first large new liner since the *QE2* she was also to introduce a quantum change in design approach, with the introduction of post-*QE2* features such as a predominance of veranda cabin accommodations on the upper decks for the first time aboard a vessel, designed to withstand the rigours of continuous express service on the North Atlantic. In view of the added height of the hull's sides needed for North Atlantic service, the cabins and suites were arranged above and below a secondary central run of public rooms atop the hull, with the three strata of accommodations below having verandas protected behind openings in the hull's sides. The main suite of public spaces below these, including a spectacular triple-height main restaurant and a fully-functional planetarium with a retractable projection dome, was laid out on a grand scale following a grand central promenade plan inspired by the *Normandie*.

Architecturally, the new ship showed little of the *QE2*'s original crisp clean-lined modernity, which had by then, bit by bit, been gradually whittled away from the older ship through the many refits and other changes made over the years. Some rooms had been changed completely, such as the original 736 Club discotheque and bar that had become the Queens Grill restaurant, while others such as the elegant Look Out lounge forward on Upper Deck had disappeared altogether, and the Double Room had been revamped numerous times in an effort to make it into a cabaret lounge, a purpose for which its space was never ever intended.

Because of the *QE2*'s great popularity and devoted following of regular passengers, who would ultimately want to sail aboard the new ship, there was the feeling that some of her features such as the Queens Room and the Golden Lion Pub, itself the product of a mid 1990s refit, should be brought forward at least in spirit even without the ship's original modernity. The design approach developed for the new *Queen Mary 2* also had to avoid being so different as to be difficult to adapt to later cruise ships that would inevitably be built for the Line.

The *Queen Mary 2* was completed and handed over to Cunard in late 2003 as the then largest passenger ship in the world at 148,250 tons and with a lower-berth passenger capacity of 2,620 persons. Her unique hull was designed with the great structural strength and added freeboard height above the waterline height needed for Atlantic crossings and other long sea passages at a relatively high service speed of 28.5 knots. This was achieved without compromise to the high proportion of outer and veranda cabins expected by passengers or to the wide range of deck facilities expected for cruising in temperate and tropical waters, and with the addition of a number of significant amenities and design features that would set the *QM2* apart as a truly singular ship.

By the time of Cunard's acquisition, Carnival's technical department and shipbuilding activities were organised as an entity called Carnival Corporate Shipbuilding, as a sort of one-stop service for the fleet development activities of the Corporation's various subsidiaries. By then these also included Costa Cruises, which joined the group in the year 2000 as part of an expansion into the European cruise market. Following the success of long Fantasy- and Statendam- series building programmes for the Carnival and Holland America fleets, the next generation of ships was planned so that each new series would be readily adaptable to the individual characteristics of more than one subsidiary within the group.

In essence this meant the overall hull form, structural configuration and layout, along with machinery and other technical installations, stores and baggage handling, food and beverages, hotel and housekeeping services, and crew facilities, would be identical and operationally interchangeable. This would form an underlying platform around which the exterior styling, accommodation and arrangement of passenger facilities, along with their interior architecture and styling, would be tailored to the specific needs and tastes, first of the subsidiary's fleet and product identity and then of each ship herself, preserving the individuality of character and identity for which most people find ships to be so irresistibly interesting.

This approach was applied with the Spirit series of four large standard-market ships built in Finland, of which she and the *Costa Atlantica* and the *Carnival Spirit* were the first to be delivered in the years 2000 and 2001 respectively. In all, six 2,142-passenger 85,820-ton ships were built in this series of which four went to Carnival and two to Costa. These were designed to a new Panamax-max standard with maximum dimensions allowing them the flexibility to squeeze through the Panama Canal.

Meanwhile, Carnival's more upscale Vista class made its first appearance in 2002 as Holland America's 81,769-ton *Zuiderdam*, with spacious luxury accommodations for 1,848 passengers in lower berths. Quite significantly, this ship was also aimed at attracting a younger clientele to luxury cruising, with a greater range of public facilities in lighter and brighter colours, reflecting more choice but still keeping the established Holland America sense of intimacy and sense of luxury. The Dutch firm VFD Interiors, which had handled the interior design of the Line's ships since the *Nieuw Amsterdam* and *Noordam* in the early 1980s, was again commissioned for the new Vista ships.

Initially, five ships were ordered in the series for completion between 2002 and 2005, of which the fourth was originally earmarked to go to Cunard as a first fleet mate for the *Queen Mary 2*. This allocation was made well before the *QM2*'s completion at a time when contracts had already been signed for the Vista ship's interior design and outfitting, and steel, machinery and other major items already ordered for her building. It was eventually decided that more time was needed to tailor the new ship to Cunard's own style of service and other specific requirements, as well as to have time to assess the *QM2*'s performance in service and to determine which of her features would win the greatest public appeal and be most suitable for adaptation to the new Cunard ship.

The fourth Vista ship was allocated instead to P&O Cruises, which had then just come into the fold through a 2003 merger of Carnival Corporation and P&O Princess Cruises, and was completed in 2005 as the *Arcadia*. She differed outwardly from the earlier Holland America ships of her class by way of a glass-sided pod atop the superstructure, housing various public spaces added around the funnel's base. This is in fact served to contain a convergence of the forward and aft engine uptakes to the twin funnels of the Holland America ships for the single funnels of this and the later Cunard ship where similar structures are also added. The *Arcadia* is the only Vista to have a white hull, itself alone distinguishing her perhaps more than anything else from the others.

From the outset this ship's public interiors were to have reflected a more modern design approach, reflecting some of the more contemporary elements of the *QM2*, carried out by the London-based design team that had worked with SMC and Sweden's Tillberg Design on the *QM2*. This is perhaps best realised in the triple-height elliptical lobby atrium's stark elegance. While the *Arcadia* shows a high standard of architectural design, the asymmetrical layout of her public rooms still reflects Holland America preferences, indicating that indeed more time would have been needed to realise a plan more specifically suited to Cunard's expectations.

A sixth Vista ship, 11.36 metres longer at the water line, and with additional hull strengthening of the bow and forward superstructure for occasional transatlantic crossings and other long ocean passages, was ordered for completion as Cunard's *Queen Victoria* at the end of 2007. As part of a $2bn deal with the Italian Fincantieri shipbuilding group, this was ordered along with an additional Vista ship for Holland America, completed in 2008 as *Eurodam*, with an option for one additional sister, as well as one each for Princess Cruises in the 116,000-ton Grand Princess series and a new larger 130,000 version of the Carnival Destiny series, eclipsing the already larger Carnival Conquest series measure of 110,239 tons and greater length of 290 metres. These were delivered as Holland America's *Eurodam*, and the *Emerald Princess* and *Carnival Dream* in 2007 and 2009 respectively. The options were taken up as *Ruby Princess* in 2008 and *Nieuw Amsterdam* to come into service later in 2010.

With added time available for planning and design, Cunard was able to pursue an approach with greater emphasis on the Line's rich history and tradition. The name *Queen Victoria* makes a connection with the Victorian era during which the Cunard Line was born and flourished through a period of great growth and development. The *Queen Victoria* was a name originally favoured for Cunard's first Queen liner in the 1930s, as it fitted the Line's convention of naming its passenger ships after old Roman provinces ending with the letters 'ia'. Legend has it though, that when King George V was asked for his consent to naming the new Cunarder for 'Britain's greatest Queen,' he apparently replied that his wife would be delighted with that, and the ship ended up accordingly being launched as the *Queen Mary*.

Where Heritage Trails had been worked into the *QE2*'s extensive Project Lifestyle refit in the mid 1990s, and included in the decoration of the *QM2* as permanent exhibitions of various historical artefacts and memorabilia, the new ship's architecture would itself make the connection with direct references to the liner era. This would be emphasised with greater recourse to the double and triple-height public spaces of the old Queens, and of the second *Mauretania* and the distinctive 1949-built *Caronia* that captured the travelling public's imagination during the early post-World War II period, before the luxury trade started taking to the jet airways in the late 1950s. Yet the new ship's design leitmotif would also look farther back from this era to the earlier influences of *Aquitania*, The Ship Beautiful, to the first *Mauretania*, and beyond to other relevant historical influences on land as well as at sea. The idea was that rather than trying to copy these influences they should be adapted as a sort of theatrical setting or scenography for their enjoyment within the context of twenty-first century luxury travel and living, in settings that are evocative of the liner era and the age of grand-luxe travel and hospitality.

Other changes from the original Vista-series plan, developed for primarily American-based cruising, would reflect a more British approach to the lifestyle amenities offered with, for instance, greater emphasis on ballroom dancing and the style of entertainment and leisure activities preferred by Britons at sea. With the ship being built and financed entirely by private enterprise, there would be no questions asked about the choices of interior design schemes in Parliament and no recommendations offered by the Design Council or the architectural and interior design professions, with Cunard and Carnival and their partners being left entirely free to make their own choices for the type of ship they really wanted to have.

If Cunard had wanted a new corporate parent or sponsor willing to invest in the large-scale fleet redevelopment programme they needed to remain competitive in twenty-first century upscale cruising. They could have done no better than to be a part of Carnival Corporation and a client of Carnival Corporate Shipbuilding's extensive sphere of activity.

*Top: In September 2017 it was announced that third 'Vista class' ship would be built for Cunard in Italy, she will join **Queen Mary 2**, **Queen Victoria** and **Queen Elizabeth** in 2022. (Cunard)*

*Above: The **Queen Mary 2** undergoing her £90m refit in Hamburg during 2016. (Cunard)*

CHAPTER 2

Designing and building the Queen Victoria

Much of what is done in the art of designing and building ships, even those of the greatest prestige and highest degree of luxury, is by reference to other vessels that are already built, are proven in service and of specific interest to the owners and operators. Part of the early planning work involves identifying specific reference ships, upon which is rooted just about anything from the overall dimensions and hull form, speed and carrying capacity, through to choices of propulsion machinery, auxiliary systems and various technical and behind the scenes services, to the layout of passenger spaces, and in particular the details of the cabins and suites and all that their outfitting and equipping entails. The ultimate success of this approach lies in the degree of success with which the influence of reference ships is shaped and tailored to assert a unique character and identity for the new ship.

In a series-building scheme such as the Vista, upon which the *Queen Victoria* is based, the overall enclosing envelope of hull and superstructure are for the most part already quite literally cast in steel. Some overall lengthening of the hull is possible, as was done for the *Queen Victoria*. There is also a degree of flexibility to alter various details of the superstructure mass and configuration, the funnels and other structures without changing the shipyard tooling and fabrication processes already in place for the series as a whole.

Vista already offered the sort of solid deep-sea liner stance Cunard needed for the *Queen Victoria*, by virtue of the size and structural stamina needed for Holland America's worldwide cruising programmes. The freeboard height of the hull's sides from the waterline to the open promenade beneath the lifeboats encloses a full four decks behind solid steel plating, with openings only for windows and a few access hatches. This is one deck higher than for some other ships of similar size designed for service over shorter distances in

*Top: The **Queen Victoria**'s first hull block is suspended from a gantry crane above the building dock awaiting its ceremonial lowering as the modern equivalent of the traditional keel laying. (Fincantieri)*

*Above: The **Queen Victoria** receives her aft-most section of the double bottom with the propulsion pod emplacements lowered into position. (Fincantieri)*

Top: The **Queen Victoria***'s structural assembly nears completion as the entire Commodore Club enclosure is lifted atop the navigating bridge. (Fincantieri)*

Above: The **Queen Victoria** *in her final stages of construction. (Pascal Baetens)*

predominantly tropical waters. The dark colour of this in both the Holland America ships and *Queen Victoria* also conveys more the visual expression of a deep-sea liner than of a tropical ship. Forward of the lifeboats, the hull's solid shell plating is carried upwards to the deck above and extended completely around the bow mooring deck, adding to the classic liner look of greater height and structural strength.

The liner profile, and indeed performance at sea, of the *Queen Victoria* also benefits from the added 11.36 metres of her overall length. As is usually done when stretching in a series build, the greater length of the *Queen Victoria* was gained by inserting an additional block in the centre-body of the hull, in much the same way that the aviation industry inserts a fuselage plug ahead of the wing spar to gain the added carrying capacity in the stretched variant of a particular aircraft type. The *Queen Victoria*'s added section, which corresponds exactly to the combined 2.8-metre widths of four standard cabins, is in fact inserted just ahead of the forward machinery space and the engine control room, approximately where the outer panoramic lifts are located in the original Holland American Vista ships.

The *Queen Victoria*'s added section is difficult to identify by sight, thanks to an overall smoothing out of her exterior lines, with the panoramic outward-facing lifts of the Holland America ships being replaced by an internal lift- and stair-tower at the ship's centre line to achieve greater flexibility in the layout of larger deluxe cabins and suites on the accommodation decks. The upper accommodation decks were extended farther astern, shortening the afterdecks terracing to also increase the overall amount of internal accommodation space. The overall aesthetic effect of these changes was to strengthen the horizontal visual impact of the ship's form as an ocean liner. As such, the *Queen Victoria*, with her distinctive big stocky *QE2* diesel-era-style Cunard funnel and other unique features, is arguably the most attractive of the Vista ships and a worthy and compatible fleet mate for the *Queen Mary 2*.

Internally, the *Queen Victoria* differs from her Vista and Signature counterparts mainly in the layout and style of her public rooms. While the catering facilities and other services retain the same location and extent as aboard the Holland America ships, the public spaces on Decks 2 and 3 otherwise follow a more direct and open plan, with generally larger spaces, and a number of these extending through the full height of both decks. The open promenade surrounding these is improved, with more space for strolling and for traditional wood-frame deckchairs with comfortable cushions and pillows thanks to space-saving refinements to the lifeboat davits and other handling equipment. The sleeping accommodations offer a greater variety of larger luxury cabins and suites, most of which are in the added mid-body section and along the length of Deck 7, two levels below the main run of topside public facilities.

Below the waterline, the original Vista engine configuration with five diesel-alternators and an auxiliary gas turbine generator set was changed to an all-diesel-electric aggregate with the turbine's location in the forward engine room being taken up by the sixth diesel. The ship is propelled by two steerable engine pods suspended beneath the ship's stern. These do away with conventional long propeller shafts and the steel bossings that enclose them from where they protrude outside the hull to the propeller brackets beneath the stern. Without the need for these and the inherent inertia from them, and power absorbed by their supporting thrust bearings and the watertight glands at their outer ends, a considerably smaller and more efficient modern electric motor can be housed directly inside the pod itself with a controllable-pitch propeller directly driven from its armature. As the pods are turnable, there is also no need for a heavy conventional rudder and its supporting stock.

Grand Lobby's lighting scheme features a large art deco opal glass central ceiling lumiere surrounded by spotlights in an arrangement reflecting the curvilinear lines of the stairways and atrium space. (Mike Louagie)

The Queen Victoria's Grand Lobby is shown here from its forward stair landing between 2 and 3 Decks looking aft towards John McKenna's bronze bas relief of the ship. (Mike Louagie)

Azipods, as these are called in an abbreviation of azimuthing pod, were first introduced aboard large passenger ships in 1998 with the Carnival Elation, second to last in their Fantasy series. These are now widely adopted throughout the cruise industry. The *Queen Mary 2* uses four of these, two azimuthing and two fixed to achieve her transatlantic service speed of 28.5 knots.

The *Queen Victoria*'s construction officially got underway with a keel laying ceremony held near Venice at the Marghera Yard of Italy's Fincantieri shipbuilders on 19th May 2006, when the first 325-ton section of the ship's hull was lowered into position in the dry dock where she was to be assembled. The first steel had been cut and construction of the various blocks making up the hull and superstructure already started some months earlier. On 15th January 2007 the building dock was flooded and *Queen Victoria* floated free in her natural medium for the first time, being towed to the fitting-out dock for completion. During the final stages of her outfitting, sea trials were run in the Adriatic during August. The *Queen Victoria* was completed and handed over to Cunard on 24th November, in time to keep her appointment with the Duchess of Cornwall and Prince of Wales for her naming ceremony in Southampton on 10th December.

Meanwhile the all-important task of designing the *Queen Victoria*'s numerous public spaces and individual accommodations was being co-ordinated and executed by the Genoese architect Giacomo Mortola and Teresa Anderson, architect and Vice President of Interior Design for Princess Cruises. With P&O Princess bringing another well-established and highly successful luxury cruise brand into the Carnival fold, care had to be taken to maintain the separate identities of both. Princess would continue to retain a more cosmopolitan international feel to its ships, while Cunard would develop the more traditional style of product to which it had long aspired.

Top: A view into the Café Carinthia from the Chart Room alongside the Queens Room mezzanine starboard on 3 Deck. (Mike Louagie)

Above: Cunard historical artefacts displayed in a vitrine on the Royal Arcade as part of the Cunard Heritage Trail. (Mike Louagie)

*The **Queen Victoria** underway at speed in the English Channel. (FotoFlite)*

*Top: The **Queen Victoria**, looking into the signature Chart Room Bar from the Royal Arcade where it passes the Queens Room mezzanine on 3 Deck. (Mike Louagie)*

Above: Another view of the Chart Room Bar which is arranged sidewalk-café style with only low balustrades separating it from the Royal Promenade and Queens Room mezzanine, opposite. (Mike Louagie)

With Princess having already built its Sun and Grand series in Italy, there was already continuity with Carnival's working relationship with Fincantieri and its design and technical departments. Anderson and Mortola had already designed the interiors for these and other Princess ships, and it was decided that the flexibility of their work was adaptable to also encompassing a suitable approach for the new Cunard ship. At the same time, Anderson and Mortola were also to work with *QM2* architects SMC Design and Designteam on the interiors of the *Ventura* and *Azura*, as a modified version of the Grand series for the British-market P&O fleet.

Today's approach to designing interiors for the hospitality industry, including ships, is to create rather than copy. Only an altogether new design scheme can make the best use of contemporary structures that enclose it, modern materials available to the designer and decorator, and above all the current living expectations of those who inhabit and use the spaces. A specific period style or other leitmotif can then be asserted within the scheme as a theatrical scenography to stimulate the desired atmosphere or ambience for the interior's use and enjoyment. The underlying new scheme takes into account the presence of the contemporary grid plan, technical facilities such as air-conditioning, wiring, plumbing, access for the disabled, emergency egress, and perhaps above all, modern architectural lighting.

The spaces themselves, and their use, are entirely different today – where the old Queens had a lounge, smoking room, library, card room and a small shop for each of their three passenger classes, today's passenger ships must provide elaborate theatres or cabaret lounges for staging full-production live entertainment, casinos and extensive shopping arcades, discotheques and alternative specialty restaurants and Internet cafés, as well as a vast array of sports and recreational facilities including elaborate spas, pools and lido decks never even contemplated for liners built two or three generations ago. The decorative leitmotif added in ships built in our own times, even where these may reproduce items from, for instance, the *Aquitania* or *Queen Mary*, is secondary to functionality and becomes largely a matter of detail. In the end it is the detail, both in the architectural scheme itself and in added moveable and soft furnishings, as well as the artwork, that determines the ultimate quality of the finished scheme and perceived authenticity of its style.

While those of us old enough to recall details of the old Cunard Queens and other liners still in service during the 1960s, let alone the *Aquitania*, which was withdrawn from service in 1950, are a dwindling minority, these ships are nonetheless still well known to the general public. The great amount of publicity they attracted continues to flourish through countless books, films and other material about them, including the highly authentic reproduction of *Titanic* for Leonardo di Caprio's blockbuster 1997 motion picture of the same name. While a whimsical portrayal of these suffices on stage for a musical or theatrical production, or to some degree even in a mass-market hospitality or cruise ship setting, the sense of fidelity and authenticity demanded in the portrayal of these is highest in the premium upscale market that is served exclusively by Cunard and but a handful of others. The setting of a traditional theme in these circumstances must also go beyond mere architecture and design to also become part of the on-board experience with added touches of personal and individual service that are themselves appropriate to today's lifestyles and perceptions of exceptional service.

As part of the unique and memorable experience the *Queen Victoria* offers, passengers have the opportunity to learn the Olympic sport of foil fencing taught by qualified instructors from the British Fencing Association, with real swords and all the necessary safety and protective equipment provided for those wanting to participate. Most remarkably

Top: The Champagne Bar, now a Cunard signature feature first introduced aboard the **Queen Mary 2**, *is adjacent to the Café Carinthia as seen in the background. (Mike Louagie)*

Above: The Queens Room, decorated for the ship's inaugural Christmas season as seen from its rear entrance point off the Royal Arcade's lower gallery on 2 Deck. (Mike Louagie)

*Top: The **Queen Victoria**'s alternative-dining Todd English Restaurant, located port side of the Grand Lobby atrium on 2 Deck, follows the introduction of the Todd English experience aboard **QM2**. (Mike Louagie)*

*Above: The **Queen Victoria**, a partial view of the Britannia Restaurant, looking along the room's starboard side. (Mike Louagie)*

though, rather than being held in a gymnasium, fencing aboard the *Queen Victoria* is carried out in surroundings that more befit this elegant sport on the polished inlaid-wood dance floor of the Queens Room. Responding to the interest Cunard passengers have shown in learning and understanding through the Line's Connexions programme, operated in association with leading universities, theatrical performances and instructional workshops are given aboard the *Queen Victoria* by leading theatrical and professional groups.

The *Queen Victoria*'s designers made extensive studies of the old Cunard liners, the original Queens, *Aquitania* and *Mauretania* as well as other ships of relevant style such as the White Star Line's 1911 *Olympic*, a near contemporary of *Aquitania* and sister ship of *Titanic* and the lesser-known *Britannic* lost during World War I before she had any opportunity to go into commercial service. Steamship company brochures were also used to get an idea of how ships such as these were presented to the travelling public. Teresa Anderson also sought references and inspiration from various hotels, private clubs and theatres in London, as well as country houses, National Trust and other heritage properties. Perhaps most significant among these was Queen Victoria and Albert's summer home, Osborne House, on the Isle of Wight.

While the *Queen Victoria* has a generous number of significant double and triple-height interiors, among them the library and shopping arcade, these needed to be given a unique treatment in the more traditional spirit of Cunard's background, and the British establishments associated with it, to differentiate these from the more contemporary feel of high-ceilinged spaces aboard other recently built upscale ships in the Holland America, Celebrity and P&O/Princess fleets. Here the designers have stressed art nouveau and deco references that can be rendered in the scale of these spaces, along with the same genuine traditional materials and

The **Queen Victoria**, looking into the Britannia Restaurant from its entrances on 2 and 3 Deck, one has a vista of the room's double-height central nave and the art deco sculptured centrepiece behind the Captain's table. (Mike Louagie)

*The **Queen Victoria**'s double-height Royal Arcade court looking forward from in front of the casino (to the left out of view) towards its processional staircase and Big Ben standard clock. (Mike Louagie)*

craftsmanship that graced Cunard interiors as much as a century ago, with wrought-iron banister railings and a wide variety of empire veneers, as these were called in the days of the old Queens, marble claddings and flooring. The fire-retardant veneers are especially made to meet today's stringent safety standards for shipboard use. The claddings are but a thin wafer of genuine Travertine marble bonded to a metal backing to reduce weight without compromising the stone's normal strength and rigidity.

Among the *Queen Victoria*'s most notable interiors is the Grand Lobby, the ship's main entrance and principal atrium, extending up from Deck 1 through the two levels of main public rooms above. It is here that embarking passengers get their all-important first impression of the ship and the voyage they are about to enjoy aboard her. The grand staircase leading to the deck above is inspired by the *Olympic*'s oak and wrought-iron staircase, where its uppermost flights ascended from a glass-domed mezzanine-plan hall forward of the first-class public rooms to the boat deck above. The *Olympic* stairway's already dramatic effect is enhanced, and brought up to the *Queen Victoria*'s larger scale, with the placing of a grotto and clock on the wall above its landing, taken in the new ship by a large Roman arch extending two-and-a-half decks up from the stair landing to the atrium's ceiling, surrounding a deco-style bronze bas-relief of the ship on a globe with a compass rose at its base and radiant sunburst above.

Created by artist John McKenna this, and a similar work in the atrium aboard the *Queen Mary 2,* was inspired by MacDonald Gill's famous map mural with its clock, sunburst and tiny animated models of the Queens showing their positions on the North Atlantic that adorns the old *Queen Mary*'s main dining room to this day, in her now static role in Long Beach, California. To achieve this effect, the stairway connecting the atrium's two upper levels is cantilevered

Top: The **Queen Victoria**, *another view of the Royal Arcade Court, seen here from the 3 Deck gallery. (Mike Louagie)*

Above: The **Queen Victoria**, *performers and stage crew prepare for an evening show in the ship's Royal Court Theatre, itself a virtually full-scale London theatre extending up through the height of 1, 2 and 3 Decks. (Mike Louagie)*

Top: The **Queen Victoria**, *inside the glass-roofed Winter Garden looking towards the ship's starboard side, with part of the open-air Pavilion Pool lido visible through the sliding doors to the left. (Mike Louagie)*

Above: The **Queen Victoria**'s *Commodore Club offers panoramic views forward and to either side of the ship from the forward end of 10 Deck, a full two decks above the navigating bridge. (Mike Louagie)*

above the forward end of the atrium opening from where the scene can be enjoyed from various heights. Above, the atrium is crowned by a shallow dome with a large central deco-style glass light fixture.

On boarding the *Queen Victoria* one becomes immediately immersed in the warm hues of the Grand Lobby's rich mahogany panelling and the earth tones of its carpeting and upholstered furnishings, seen in the glow of electric light filtered through the dome's opal glass fixtures and from accenting spotlights. It is a sensation that evokes first impressions of the old Cunard Queens, and for the vast majority of passengers today who have never experienced this first hand, at least the same feeling is conveyed by all those remarkable sepia-tone photographs of these ships that have stirred their imaginations through the last three generations.

Forward of the Grand Lobby's upper two levels and beyond the Queens Room, the Royal Arcade, also panelled in rich veneers and with wrought-iron balustrades, is inspired by London's classically chic Burlington and Queen's Opera Arcades, with the bay-windowed design of its shop fronts reflecting the classic style of these elegant London passages. The central open atrium area and processional staircase, however, also show the influence of the 1920s and 1930s mezzanine-plan ocean liner ballrooms and lounges. The majority of shops are arranged around the mezzanine, following a similar plan from the *QE2*'s Double Room upper level so rearranged as part of her first major refit in 1972. The Royal Arcade's lower level encompasses the Empire Casino, with the Golden Lion Pub enclosed under the starboard mezzanine. Here, at the centre of the stairway, is a standard clock with Westminster Chimes from Dent & Company who made the great four-faced tower clock of the Houses of Parliament in Westminster whose famed Big Ben bell has chimed the hours in London for more than 130 years, and is internationally known to radio listeners of the BBC World Service.

The Queens Room has now become an institution aboard Cunard's ships, following its appearance first aboard the *QE2* as her first-class main lounge. Brought forward both to the *QM2* and now to the *Queen Victoria*, this serves mainly as a hotel-style ballroom for the 'black and white' balls, with gentlemen attired in tuxedos or dinner jackets and ladies in formal long gowns that reflect the British love of ballroom dancing and have also become a prominent feature of the social life aboard Cunard's ships. With the flat surface of a large dance floor, a stage and ample seating, the Queens Room serves a variety of other functions for everything from receptions, daytime entertainment, afternoon tea, fashion shows and parties, to passport inspection, immigration formalities and other such processing of passengers where these are carried out aboard ship prior to disembarkation. On other ships these procedures all too often have to be handled in cabaret lounges where passengers must queue on sloped or terraced floors and then ascend stairs to the stage proscenium for processing.

The *Queen Victoria*'s Queens Room draws inspiration from Osborne House, where the colonnaded loggia and upper gallery along the room's starboard and aft sides is inspired by similar features forming a loggia and musicians' gallery along one side of the palace's ornate Durbar Room, its name derived from the Hindi word darbar, meaning court. Designed as a state banquet hall and ballroom, the Indian themed Durbar Room is part of the new Main Wing, housing accommodations for the royal household, council and audience, added to the house in 1890–1891. The reference to Osborne House is very appropriate for the new Cunard ship, as it was *Queen Victoria*'s favourite residence from the time of its acquisition early in her reign until she returned to the Isle of Wight to live out the last days of her long and illustrious life.

Top: The **Queen Victoria***, the domed circular Hemispheres lounge on 10 Deck is one of the ship's more modern and high tech spaces. (Mike Louagie)*

Above: The **Queen Victoria***, another view of the Princess Grill interior at the room's forward end. (Mike Louagie)*

The **Queen Victoria**, seen here is the Princess Grill restaurant, located highest in the ship at the funnel's base on 11 Deck, looking aft inside the room. (Mike Louagie)

54

The Queens Room is adorned with a portrait of Victoria as the young Queen-Empress painted by Italian-born New York artist Giancarlo Impiglia, already familiar for his works aboard Cunard's other Queens. Most notable among these are his more abstract, contemporary, brightly colourful depictions of life aboard imaginary cruise ships in murals aboard the *QE2* and *QM2*. His latest work aboard the *Queen Victoria* is quite different from these in that it is a more scholarly nineteenth-century-style portrait from an age before photography, rather than the situation depictions where the characters are virtually featureless. Impiglia made a thorough study of nineteenth-century portraits of the young Victoria enabling him to develop an entirely new image of her for his work, which is itself a return to the time of his own art studies in Rome.

Apart from its architectural references to the Durbar Room's loggia and gallery, decoration of the *Queen Victoria*'s Queens Room is generally of a light and elegant liner style, perhaps recalling ocean-going styles of the 1930s, with its use of light maple veneers, gold-leaf ornamentation and backlit stained-glass murals. Designed as a primarily inside space, flanked by the Royal Gallery's extension on one side and with windows in the opposite ship's side only on its main level, the two large crystal chandeliers above the dance floor are the main light source, along with the indirect lighting of the coffered ceiling surrounding them. The raised seating areas in the loggias to either side of the dance floor, and the starboard side gallery above, are arranged for optimum viewing of the large dance floor in a style, recalling the Grand Hotel experience of a century ago as it would have been in the Dorchester or London Ritz Carlton.

Across the forward end of Decks 1, 2 and 3 is the Royal Court Theatre, serving as the *Queen Victoria*'s main entertainment venue. Unlike many American-based cruise ships where the main show place is in fact a Las Vegas-style cabaret lounge, designed for revue-style variety shows, with cocktail tables and bar service provided for the audience, the 830-seat Royal Court Theatre is styled after the London West End and Broadway commercial theatres of the early twentieth century, geared to a lighter genre of dramatic, comedic and music-hall shows aimed at the broader spectrum of the population in large cities such as London and New York.

A key feature of the Royal Court Theatre's ornately decorated auditorium is the inclusion of 16 private boxes at its two upper levels. Apart from the novelty of offering a feature such as this at sea, is the way in which those booking the boxes are given a special experience when attending the performance. The idea is for them to be personally escorted by the ship's liveried bellboys from the restaurant after dinner, to special reception lounges behind the boxes at either side of the theatre for dessert and pre-show champagne, before being ushered to their private boxes. It is touches such as these that, as much as anything else, contribute to the passenger's real sense of an exclusive luxury cruise experience. Unreserved boxes are made available to others on a first-come-first-served basis immediately before the show.

The library, tucked in behind the port-side lifts amidships, is one of the ship's smaller double-decker spaces, with its mezzanine plan, open spiral staircase and backlit stained-glass dome at its centre. It bears the design influence of London's many exclusive private clubs, or perhaps even the academic surroundings of a college at Oxford or Cambridge Universities. Apart from the split-level arrangement of the old *Queen Elizabeth*'s library, this is the only Cunard ship to have a multi-level library, and is rivalled in today's cruise fleets only by Celebrity's Millennium series ships. The *Queen Victoria*'s library's collection of 6,000 volumes is supplemented with audio books and other modern electronic media.

Top: The **Queen Victoria**, a view into the Grill Terrace court located between the Princess and Queens Grill restaurants looking towards the Princess Grill to starboard. (Mike Louagie)

Above: The **Queen Victoria**, a soup servery in the Lido Restaurant on 9 Deck, showing the room's decorative tiled wall paintings. (Mike Louagie)

The main Britannia Restaurant at the aft end of Decks 2 and 3 follows the overall Vista layout, with panoramic windows on three sides, though with a smaller opening between its upper and lower levels so as to increase the dining area itself. Upon entering the room one has an axial vista along its double-height nave towards a large deco sculpture in bronze and glass of Cunard's rampant lion and the globe from the Line's house flag, set into a freestanding panel as a backdrop to the Captain's table. The style of this too is reminiscent of MacDonald Gill's mural in the old *Queen Mary*'s first-class dining room. Without being exclusively of any particular style, the room is otherwise representative of various influences evoking the liner era and age of grand-luxe travel as a background setting for enjoyment of the *Queen Victoria*'s gastronomy. While many cruise lines in the standard market are moving away from formal dining with fixed table assignments and meal times, Cunard continues to stress a single sitting for lunch and dinner times, and assigned table seating fostering a more personal relationship between passengers and the restaurant staff who thus look after them throughout the voyage.

As aboard the *QM2* those occupying premium-grade cabins and suites are served in the exclusive Princess and Queens Grill restaurants located on their own deck high above the ship, along with the private Grill Lounge. These rooms all offer a panoramic outlook from full-height widows looking out to the horizon at either side, and forward over the ship's open decks below. They are grouped around a small central enclosed court, open to the sky above where outdoor alfresco service is available in warm weather.

The *Queen Victoria* reflects Cunard's strong emphasis on food and beverage services, firmly rooted in Cunard's traditional liner services. During the earlier liner era, apart from ballroom dancing to music played by the ship's orchestra and improvised film shows in the lounge,

The **Queen Victoria**, *a vintage painting of Cunard's first Mauretania (1907-35) with her hull in "cruising white" of her latter years in service adorned a wall in the Churchill's Admiral's Lounge on 10 Deck. (Mike Louagie)*

The **Queen Victoria** off the coast of Kent en route to Southampton. (FotoFlite)

Queen Victoria
SOUTHAMPTON

*The **Queen Victoria** emerges through early-morning fog, brand new on her first in-service port of call at Rotterdam Europoort on 12th December 2007. (Mike Louagie)*

passengers otherwise were left to their own devices to pass the long days at sea. Meal times were thus events of the day to be looked forward to as much as for being significant social occasions as for enjoyment of the gastronomy itself. Cunard has long prided itself on the quality and variety of its cuisine – a passenger's request for bacon at breakfast on the old Queens, for instance, would bring the inevitable steward's response, 'What kind Sir / Madam' – there were three to choose from. Dining aboard the *Queen Mary 2* and *Queen Victoria* is still special among the broader range of activities and diversions these ships offer, reflecting the current trends of five-star hotelier haut cuisine, featuring both British and international specialties.

The emphasis is as much on diversity as it is on the quality of food and service. The Britannia Restaurant retains the traditional liner-era institution of a formal à la carte dinner service each evening with two fixed sittings, though with breakfast and lunch offered on a more informal open seating basis. Alternatively, passengers can dine al fresco in the Lido Café at breakfast and lunch times and choose a reserved-seating bistro-style evening dining experience featuring cuisine from different parts of the world each evening. Traditional British pub grub such as fish and chips, toad in the hole and bangers and mash, never offered aboard the old Queens, is featured in the Golden Lion Pub, from its own kitchen with the necessary deep fryers and other equipment for this culinary genre. At the higher end of the scale is the exclusive cover-charge Todd English Restaurant serving the renowned American celebrity chef's nouveau and Mediterranean cuisine in the characteristic opulence of his establishments ashore.

Dining aboard the *Queen Victoria* also retains a vestigial legacy of the three-class service aboard the old Cunard Queens, though here it is in effect first class, first plus and first plus plus, based on the wide range of cabin and suite grades. The Queens and Princess Grill Restaurants cater exclusively at two levels to those occupying the ship's premium-grade cabins and suites. In addition to the impeccable à la carte service and individual cuisine of these restaurants, passengers in the 'Grill' classes can dine al fresco in the sheltered open-air courtyard between the two Grill restaurants.

Also among the *Queen Victoria*'s upper decks public rooms is the Commodore Club, overlooking the ship's bow from a vantage point high above the navigating bridge, offering the same compelling vistas over the ship's bow as did the forward-facing cocktail bars aboard Cunard's old Queens three-quarters of a century ago. The *Queen Mary 2* introduced the Commodore Club as a more contemporary take on this, reflecting the *QE2*'s original Look Out lounge before it disappeared as a victim of her 1972 refit. Despite its modern features of wraparound panoramic windows on three sides and raised central bar area for optimum advantage of the outlook, this newest interpretation goes back to even earlier traditions in its decoration and furnishings, with high-back winged club chairs, leather upholstery, brass fittings and rich dark veneers. It is adjoined by the similarly styled Admiral's Club and Churchill's Cigar Lounge. Aft of these and the forward main stair-tower is the circular-plan Hemispheres, serving as a flexible venue for various daytime activities, before becoming an elegant nightclub after dark. With its perforated bright metal sphere set into a sectioned glazed screen at the room's entrance, providing both privacy and a central focal point to the interior, this is probably the most contemporary public space aboard the *Queen Victoria*.

CHAPTER 3

TheQueen Victoria makes her debut

At 11:00 am on 24th November 2007, the Italian flag was lowered from the *Queen Victoria*'s mast and the Red Ensign run up in its place while the ship changed nationality and ownership as she was officially handed over from her builders to her owners at Fincantieri's Marghera yard. Later that day, after the dignitaries and guests invited for the handover had left and final preparations for sea were completed, the second largest ship ever built for Cunard after the *Queen Mary 2* sailed for her new home and port of registry at Southampton, arriving there a week later to be prepared for her official naming ceremony and service debut.

Naming ceremonies have now taken the place of traditional launchings, when she would be named by some prominent person, usually a lady, chosen to do the honours.

A bottle of champagne would be swung by hand against the bow and, as it shattered, a lever pulled to, symbolically at least, release the launch mechanism setting hull in motion, sliding down from its inclined building ways into the water as thousands of shipyard workers cheered and tossed their caps into the air. These events were always a dramatic celebration of human industrial endeavour that, alas, has since given way to the rationale of more modern ways.

Today's ships are block-built from already-assembled sections of the hull and superstructure, weighing several hundred tons apiece, that are precisely aligned along the bottom of a dry dock and attached to one another by automated electric-arc-welding equipment. The baptism comes when the ship is floated free as the dock is flooded and she is manoeuvred by tugs to a fitting-out quay for the

*The **Queen Victoria** is given a traditional fireboat welcome on her maiden approach to Southampton Docks as she arrives in England from Fincantieri. (Andrew Cooke)*

*The **Queen Victoria** lies alongside the City Cruise Terminal in the Port of Southampton's Western Docks in readiness for her naming ceremony. (Andrew Cooke)*

completion of her upper decks and funnel and other outer structures, the stepping of her main mast and outfitting of her interiors. The floating out is usually marked by a small shipyard ceremony, with the traditional launch celebration in effect replaced by a naming ceremony performed at the new ship's home port after she is completed and handed over to her owners. The already-known name is unveiled by the ship's Godmother, as the officiating lady is now known, and a jeroboam of champagne shattered against the hull plating. The poignancy of such celebrations today is heightened by a sense of the ship's belonging to the home port, from where she will sail, and where there is a sense of her belonging to the town or city and its populace, some of whom probably at least will sail with her as officers and crew.

The *Queen Victoria*'s naming ceremony in Southampton occurred almost four years after the same honours were performed there for her French-built older sister, the *Queen Mary 2*. The venue was, however, changed from the Ocean Dock to the City Cruise Terminal, where spectators would have a better view of the ship and the outdoor festivities from nearby Mayflower Park, where they would be unencumbered by security restrictions on access to the port itself.

A full day of festivities both ashore and on board was highlighted by the 3:30 pm naming ceremony itself. This was held in a large temporary auditorium erected on the quayside with terraced seating to optimise viewing for 2,000 invited guests and with the stage backdrop being a glass wall through which the ship's bow could be seen. The ship was first blessed by the Bishop of Winchester with the words:

*The **Queen Victoria** is swung by the tug Svitzer Sarah in readiness to go alongside Pier 101 at the City Cruise Terminal. (Andrew Cooke)*

They that go down to the sea in ships;
That do business in great waters;
These see the works of the Lord, and His wonders in the deep.

The naming itself was performed by HRH The Duchess of Cornwall, accompanied by her husband HRH The Prince of Wales, with the traditional phrase:
'I name this ship *Queen Victoria*; May God bless all who sail upon her.'

The Duchess then pressed a button to release a magnum of Veuve Clicquot that hit the *Queen Victoria*'s port side shell plating on target but remained intact. As things such as this do happen at namings, someone was standing by with a reserve bottle that was quickly thrust down from the bow deck and did shatter with the desired effect as the *Queen Victoria*'s whistle bellowed overhead and helium-filled balloons were released into the air, also to the tumultuous applause and cheers of the official quayside party and the additional thousands who had thronged into Mayflower Park.

The ceremony included the London Philharmonic Orchestra accompanying singer Katherine Jenkins in selections from Bizet's 'Carmen', and the three tenors, Alfie Boe, Jon Christos and Gardar Thor Cortes, finishing up with a patriotic rendition of 'Rule Britannia'.

Cunard has retained a long-standing relationship with the royal family. The *Queen Mary* was launched on 26th September 1934 by her royal namesake (1867–1953) and the *Queen Elizabeth* on 27th September 1938 by hers, Elizabeth, the late Queen Mother, (1900–2002). Both ships were visited on various occasions during their long careers by the Queens who had launched them, though. HM Queen Elizabeth II launched the *Queen Elizabeth 2* on 20th September 1967 and named the *Queen Mary 2* on 8th January 2004. She and the Duke of Edinburgh have visited the *QE2* at various times during her career with a final tour of the ship

Top: Cunard President and CEO, Carol Marlow, HRH The Prince of Wales and his wife the HRH The Duchess of Cornwall at the naming ceremony. (Cunard)

Above: HRH The Duchess of Cornwall with Bell Boys from the **Queen Victoria**. *(Cunard)*

Top: The **Queen Victoria** is honoured with a spectacular firework display as she leaves Southampton on her maiden voyage. (Cunard)

Above: The **Queen Victoria**, opera singer Katherine Jenkins in performance at the concert that followed the ship's naming ceremony. (Cunard)

being made by Prince Philip on the day of her departure from Southampton to her new owners in Dubai.

Prince Charles was on the bridge of the QE2 with Cunard chairman, Sir Basil Smallpiece and Captain William Warwick 19th November 1968 when the ship departed from her Clydeside fitting-out berth under her own steam for dry-docking at Greenock. His first wife, HRH Princess Diana, named the Finnish-built cruise ship Royal Princess for P&O Princess Cruises at Southampton in 1984, and in 1987 toured the QE2, hosted a children's event on board and met with crew members from all departments following the ship's re-engining refit in Germany.

As the last guests of the naming ceremonies disembarked from the Queen Victoria the following morning, the final consignments of stores were already going aboard as the ship was made ready for work. Paying passengers embarked later that day for her first voyage, a ten-day Christmas Markets cruise to Rotterdam, Copenhagen, Oslo, Hamburg and Zeebrugge. The opportunity was also taken to showcase the Queen Victoria to the European media and travel industry, with tours of the ship, briefings, luncheons and other events arranged at each port of call. This was followed by a Christmas cruise to Madeira and the Canary Islands. Coincidentally when, after 27 years on the North Atlantic and in wartime service, the old Queen Mary made her first cruise on 23rd December 1963, this too was a round-trip Christmas excursion to the Atlantic Islands from Southampton.

On 6th January 2008 the Queen Victoria began her first around-the-world cruise, a 106-day westwards-about circumnavigation of the globe, first to New York, through the Panama Canal to Los Angeles, onwards to Hawaii, the South Pacific, South East Asia, India, Dubai, Egypt and through Suez to the Mediterranean and back home to Southampton. The first leg of the voyage, a direct winter North Atlantic

Top: The **Queen Victoria** *alongside in Southampton's Western Docks as the* **Queen Mary 2** *makes her departure in the foreground. (Cunard)*

crossing to New York was made in tandem with, and also under the perhaps motherly watch of, the veteran *QE2*. Both Queens arrived in New York on 13th January, where they were joined by the *Queen Mary 2* for the first-ever rendezvous of three Cunard Queens. The event was feted with a spectacular fireworks display against a backdrop of the Manhattan skyline and the Statue of Liberty.

The *Queen Victoria* and *QE2* were to meet again for the last time on 19th July 2008, when the two ships tied up bow to bow at Zeebrugge. The *QE2*'s sale to Istithmar investment group for redevelopment as a hotel and tourist attraction in the Palm Jumeirah beach complex in Dubai had already been announced on 18th June 2007, and the ship was halfway through her last season with Cunard. As passengers gazed up at both ships from the pier, groups of crew members from each visited those aboard the other.

At the time of writing these closing paragraphs of this book, the *Queen Victoria* has been service almost two years to the day. In Cunard's tradition of swift, regular and safe passage, she has performed without incident or mishap and has already become a successful and popular ship. She is a modern ship functionally and operationally, and is endowed with a strong sense of tradition in the style with which Cunard identifies itself.

As Christopher Rynd, who has commanded the *Queen Elizabeth 2*, *Queen Mary 2* and *Queen Victoria* explains, those of Cunard's loyal following who came to the *Queen Victoria* with the feeling that nothing could ever compare with their beloved *QE2* are pleased and well satisfied with the experience the new ship offers.

CHAPTER 4

The first ten years and 2017 makeover

The *Queen Victoria* completed her third World Cruise in 2010, where she was joined by Captain Chris Wells who was aboard to familiarise himself with the 'Vista class' ship after his command of the *Queen Mary 2*, he later took command of *Queen Elizabeth* in late 2010. During a call at Sydney, the *Queen Victoria* was illuminated in pink in support of Breast Cancer Research.

On 9th December 2010, Cunard announced its first female captain, Faroese born Inger Klein Olsen, who would take command of the *Queen Victoria* from that December. She had joined Cunard in 1997 as first officer aboard the *Caronia*. Her first task as captain was to take the ship to a dry dock in Hamburg for a refit.

Two years after the first Cunard Royal Rendezvous, on the same date, *Queen Mary 2* met up with both *Queen Victoria* and *Queen Elizabeth* for another Royal Rendezvous in New York City on 13th January 2011. Both the *Queen Victoria* and *Queen Elizabeth* made a tandem crossing of the Atlantic for the event. All three ships met in front of the Statue of Liberty at 18.45 for a 'Grucci' fireworks display. The Empire State Building was lit up in red to mark the event.

Commenting on the event Peter Shanks, president of Cunard Line, said 'This is another historic occasion for Cunard and New York, marking the second time in our 171-year history that our entire fleet of Queens will meet there in such celebratory fashion, and marking *Queen Elizabeth*'s maiden call to our North America homeport. We look forward to bringing this next meeting of our Queens to the great city of New York and continuing the pageantry and grand celebration that is Cunard.'

In March 2011 the *Queen Victoria* docked close the former Cunard vessel *Queen Mary* at her permanent resting place, as a hotel, at Long Beach, California; the event was followed by a fireworks display.

A year later on 5th June 2012, all three Queens met again

Top: HRH The Duchess of Cornwall unveils a painting of herself by the artist Richard Stone. (Cunard)

*Above: The **Queen Victoria** makes her way up the Amazon on a special cruise in 2017. (Cunard)*

but this time in Southampton to celebrate the Diamond Jubilee of Queen Elizabeth II. In May 2014 all three Queens met up for the first time in Lisbon, Portugal, in preparation for *Queen Mary 2*'s 10th birthday. All three ships on departure sailed in a one-line formation to Southampton. On 9th May 2014 the *Queen Elizabeth* and *Queen Victoria* led, in single file, the *Queen Mary 2* up the Southampton water, then both ships docked in a bow-to-bow formation performing a birthday salute to *Queen Mary 2*. Later on in the day, all three sisters gather for a fireworks display.

On 25th May 2015 the three Queens were at Liverpool to celebrate 175 years of the formation of the Cunard Line, which was formed and based at Liverpool. The three ships stopped in line in the middle of the River Mersey, bow to stern, turning 180 degrees in full synchronisation with each other. The *Queen Mary 2* was in the centre with her bow in line with the Cunard Building at the Pier Head. The RAF Red Arrows performed a flypast in Vic formation, emitting red, white and blue smoke, over the vessels. An estimated 1.3 million people lined the riverbanks to witness the spectacle.

In 2017 the *Queen Victoria* made history, making her maiden voyage through the 'Meeting of Waters', to become the largest passenger ship to sail the Amazon, sailing between the dark Rio Negro and the pale Amazon River in Manaus, Brazil. Manaus marked the sixth out of 32 ports on the *Queen*

*This page and opposite page: On 25th May 2015 the **Queen Mary 2**, **Queen Victoria** and **Queen Elizabeth** saluted the city of Liverpool where Samuel Cunard began his transatlantic line in 1840. Thousands of people lined the River Mersey to watch the 'three queens' perform a synchronised sailing display. A special waterfront light show followed in the evening using the backdrop of the 'Three Graces'. (Cunard / Miles Cowsill)*

Victoria's 41,000 nautical mile, 120-night World Voyage.

The captain of the *Queen Victoria*, Peter Philpott, said, 'I feel immensely proud and privileged to be in command of *Queen Victoria* as she makes her maiden transit of the mighty Amazon River and berths at the port of Manaus, nearly 900 miles from the open ocean. The fact that a liner the size of *Queen Victoria* is able to travel so far up river demonstrates the enormous size and scale of the Amazon and for our guests on board to be able to experience Cunard's renowned White Star Service whilst they watch the spectacular scenery unfold in front of them has been truly unique.'

Three months later Cunard continued its commitment to upgrading the fleet with the announcement that the *Queen Victoria* would undergo a major refit in May. The ship would be taken out of service in May 2017 to undergo a major overhaul with the company investing over £34 million on the refit, which would be undertaken at the Fincantieri Shipyard in Palermo, Italy. The schedule for completion of the extensive overhaul would be within a month, by 4th June 2017.

The *Queen Victoria*'s art deco past would remain, however the refurbishments would bring the new higher standards now available on the other ships in the fleet. New to the *Queen Victoria* would be Britannia Club Dining, with the addition of an intimate restaurant and 43 spacious Britannia Club staterooms in a prime mid-ship location on Decks 7 and 8. The new and refreshed staterooms would feature newly-designed carpets, soft furnishings and new flat-screen TVs, as well as tea and coffee facilities. The new Britannia Club Restaurant would offer guests the flexibility to dine whenever they choose.

The ship's Grand Suites and Penthouse Suites would be completely redesigned, offering enhanced comfort. The Aquitania, Berengaria, Mauretania and Laconia Suites would have similar square footage to those on the *Queen Elizabeth*

*From left to right, the **Queen Elizabeth**, **Queen Mary 2** and **Queen Victoria** on 25th May 2015. (Cunard)*

*The **Queen Victoria** enters the dry-dock in Italy for extensive refit in May 2017. (Cunard)*

with approximately 1,436 sq. ft. Refreshed designs would include a new colour scheme that takes its inspiration from the line's history with its signature Cunard purple.

Simon Palethorpe, Senior Vice President, Cunard commenting on the investment said: 'This investment in *Queen Victoria* just goes to demonstrate Cunard's passion for delivering an experience that exceeds guests' expectations in luxury travel by sea. For the first time on *Queen Victoria*, guests can enjoy an elevated experience with large, well-appointed balcony staterooms in prime locations and the new Britannia Club Restaurant will be the perfect setting for those who prefer a more intimate dining experience in one of the finest restaurants at sea.' He went on to add, 'As part of the Queen Victoria refurbishment, we've looked to heighten our customers' experience in every way, from the extension of the aft lido sun deck to refreshed interiors across the board. Responding to the demands of our guests, we've introduced 43 Britannia Club Staterooms, bringing the *Queen Victoria* in line with the rest of the Cunard fleet. The distinctive Cunard elegance remains of course and design cues have been taken from previous Cunard ships, such as the original *Queen Mary* and *Queen Elizabeth*. At the same time, there are many enhancements – for example, new bar concepts and large flat-screen TVs in all staterooms – that meet the needs of today's luxury traveller. We're looking forward to inviting the first Cunard guests on board to enjoy the new additions and refreshed features.'

Additionally, Cunard announced a new Chart Room concept, which will debut on the *Queen Victoria* as part of the refit. The new Chart Room will be located on Deck 2 off the Grand Lobby, where Café Carinthia was located. The Chart Room will feature illy coffee, Godiva chocolate treats and light bites by day and stellar cocktails by night. Cunard will also introduce a 'gin and fizz' themed menu to the Midships Lounge, including a variety of wines, Proseccos, cavas and

Top: A rendered image of the Britannia Club restaurant which would offer dining from 6.30 and 9.00pm. (Cunard)

Above: Another rendered image of the new-look Queens Grill Aft Suite. (Cunard)

*Work starts on the **Queen Victoria**'s £34 million refit in Italy. (Cunard)*

champagnes alongside premium gins and spirits, all blended to create fresh and inspiring cocktails with a modern twist.

As part of her refit the lido sun deck was overhauled as well as the Winter Garden.

The ship was taken out of service on 5th May, sailed to the Fincantieri Shipyard in Palermo, Italy and was returned to service on 4th June. The *Queen Victoria* then embarked on her maiden four-night voyage, visiting Amsterdam and Zeebrugge (Bruges), before returning to Southampton.

The *Queen Victoria* 'World Voyage' for 2018 will be the first time that Cunard have offered a two- to three-month mid-duration 'World Voyage', which will appeal to guests looking for an exotic 'winter escape' round-trip experience that offers a mix of relaxation and exploration. The *Queen Victoria* returns to South America in 2018, this time offering more immersive destinations and visiting the major South American cities as well as offering stunning scenic cruising in the Magellan Straits, Chilean Fjords and Cape Horn. In addition to the exploration of South America, she will call at the iconic and relaxing destinations of Barbados, Jamaica and

*The new stern accomodation module is lifted onto the **Queen Victoria**. (Cunard)*

The imposing Grand Lobby on the **Queen Victoria**. (Cunard)

The Veranda Restaurant offers contemporary French cuisine. The Verandah takes design inspiration from the original Verandah Grill on board **Queen Mary**. *(Cunard)*

*Top: The library on the **Queen Victoria** is spread over two decks and linked by a wooden spiral staircase. (Cunard)*

*Above: **Queen Victoria**'s Royal Court Theatre. (Cunard)*

Left: Formerly the Hemispheres, the Yacht Club was introduced as part of 2017 refit. (Cunard)

Bermuda and will transit the Panama Canal. During her 75-night World Voyage she will sail over 22,000 nautical miles, call at 26 ports and visit 15 countries.

For her 'World Voyage' in 2019, the *Queen Victoria* will operate Cunard's only full circumnavigation for 2019 and will follow the most popular routing, the classic Western Circumnavigation via the Panama Canal. The full 107-night voyage ends with the Indian Ocean and South Africa before returning to Southampton.

Right: The Chart Room moved into the former Café Carinthia located on Deck 2 as part of the ships refit in 2017. (Cunard)

Left: The Club Britannia Restaurant. (Cunard)

Top: Another view of the Chart Room which combins modern elements with all the hallmarks of a timeless cocktail bar. (Cunard)

*Above: The '3 Queens Gin' on the **Queen Victoria**. (Cunard)*

The Lido Restaurant offers superb views on Deck 9 of the ship's passage. (Cunard)

Located in the heart of Deck 9 next to the Lido, the Winter Garden commands some of the best views across the ship and out to sea. (Cunard)

Left: The elegant Queens Room is the location for the tradition of afternoon tea, music and dancing. (Cunard)

Top: The new Godiva chocolates area is located outside the Chart Room on Deck 2. (Cunard)

Above: The Red Lion Pub. (Cunard)

Top: Looking over the Sun Deck on the **Queen Victoria***. (Cunard)*

Above: The **Queen Victoria***'s spa offers steam rooms and an exclusive pool offering complete tranquillity. The hot stone beds facing the panoramic windows offer perhaps some of the most relaxing views imaginable. (Cunard)*

QUEEN VICTORIA - CUNARD LINE

Builders:	Fincantieri, Marghera Yard, Italy		Draft:	8 m
Keel laid:	19th May 2006		Air draft (Height above waterline):	55.60 m
Floated out:	15th January 2007		Depth to bulkhead deck (A Deck):	10.80 m
Delivered:	24th November 2007		Depth to Promenade Deck (3 Deck):	19.81 m
Fincantieri Yard number:	6,127			
IMO number:	9320556		**Measure and capacities**	
Flag:	Bermuda		Gross tonnage (GT):	90,746
Port of registry:	Hamilton		Net tonnage (NT):	50,618
Classification:	Lloyd's Register +100A1		Deadweight tonnage (tDW):	7,700
			Passengers, lower berths:	2,014
Overall dimensions			Passengers, maximum:	2,218
Length overall:	294.0 m		Passenger accommodations:	1,007 cabins and suites,
Waterline length:	265.36 m		86% with outside exposure, 71% with private verandas	
Beam:	32.26 m		Officers and crew:	982

The **Queen Victoria**, *a painting by Robert Lloyd showing the ship against a background of the Venice waterfront.*

Robert·G·Lloyd 2007

Fuel capacity:	3,456 m2	Fuel consumption:	240 tonnes heavy fuel oil per 24 hours
Fresh water capacity:	3,150 m2	Manoeuvering:	2 transverse bow thrusters used in conjunction with the pods for docking

Machinery and performance

Power:	6 diesel generator sets in total generating 63,360 kW of electrical power.	Stabilization:	2 retractable anti-rolling fins
Propulsion:	2 azimuthing propeller pods yielding a total motive power of 35,200 kW		
Trial speed:	24.3 knots		
Service speed:	21.7 knots		

*The **Queen Victoria** returns to Southampton after undergoing her £34 million refurbishment in Palermo, Italy. (Cunard)*